THE INSIDER'S GUIDE TO POWER IN AUSTRALIA

by JACK *the* INSIDER

THE INSIDER'S GUIDE TO POWER IN AUSTRALIA

by JACK *the* INSIDER

AS TOLD TO **RICHARD FIDLER** AND **PETER HOYSTED**

RANDOM HOUSE AUSTRALIA

Random House Australia Pty Ltd
Level 3, 100 Pacific Highway, North Sydney, NSW 2060
www.randomhouse.com.au

Sydney New York Toronto
London Auckland Johannesburg

First published by Random House Australia 2007

National Library of Australia
Cataloguing-in-Publication Entry

Jack the Insider.
The Insider's guide to power in Australia by Jack the Insider.
ISBN 978 1 74166 689 2 (pbk.).
1. Political satire, Australian. 2. Australia – Politics and government – Humor.
I. Fidler, Richard. II. Hoysted, Peter. III. Title.
320.9940207

Cover illustration by Bill Chan and Peter Hoysted
Cover and text design by Bill Chan
Printed and bound by the BPA Print Group, Victoria

10 9 8 7 6 5 4 3 2 1

This book is dedicated to the Australian Society of Primates

With thumbs we oppose!

Pour ce que rire est le propre de l'homme

François Rabelais (1494–1553)

Contents

JACK *the* INSIDER
WHO IS HE?

JACK THE INSIDER is a man close to the top of public life in Australia. Very close to the top.

His identity cannot be fully revealed but he's got mates everywhere. Richo, Singo, Baby John Burgess; they're all mates of Jack's. And odds are, if your name ends in an 'o', and you've got a good word for Australia, then Jack is your mate too.

Jack looks back fondly to a time when Australia was much more at ease with itself: a time when kiddies could play cricket in the street, when a deal was cemented with a handshake and the coppers could run this country free from the dead hand of judicial oversight.

Jack has borne witness to some of the most glorious episodes in our nation's history.

It was Jack who poured beer over Hawkie's head after the America's Cup victory. It was Jack who egged on Sir John Kerr to say what he really thought of the protestors at the Melbourne Cup. And when John Howard lost the Liberal leadership back in '89, it was Jack who gently cradled his sobbing head.

But for all his influence and power, Jack remains a humble Aussie bloke. Every three years he does his bit for democracy: on election night it's Jack who puts the numbers on the board in the National Tally Room.

Jack maintains close links in politics, sport and business and he knows how this country really works. He's chosen to speak out frankly and fearlessly, which is why his full identity must be shrouded in the deepest secrecy.

He hates the internet.

OTHER CONTRIBUTORS

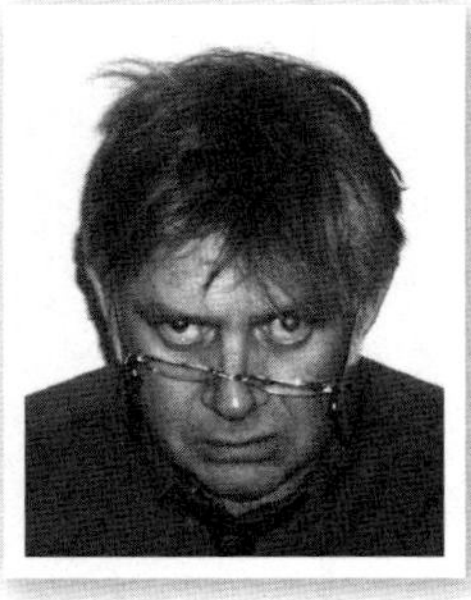

Tiberius Snatch

Beloved national dramatist, gifted poet and speechwriter for several Labor Opposition leaders

Snatch declared that politics wasn't worth the candle after Whitlam was sacked in 1975 but then hung around for the next three decades.

Tiberius Snatch knows all the secret sexual histories – the sperm lines of power in Australia. For example: were you aware that Kim Beazley Jnr is actually the son of Kim Beazley Snr? And did you know that James Packer is in fact a twelve-year-old girl?

An avid connoisseur of semen, Tiberius is often seen with several cubic centimetres of the stuff caked to his pants.

His life's work is to translate every speech in Hansard into iambic pentameter.

Tiberius is himself the father of some nineteen bastard children who have all sworn to kill him.

Libby Hyphenated-Surname

Former Liberal Party enthusiast and warrior for 'more niceness' in national debate

Hyphenated-Surname brings to this book her unique insight into the secret rituals of Australia's most successful party: the Liberals.

After narrowly missing out on preselection for a safe New South Wales seat, Hyphenated-Surname loosed the Labradors of War on the party she'd served all her adult life. At a crowded media conference she controversially insisted that senior New South Wales Liberals were deliberately ignoring evidence of a satanic paedophile network among team mascots in the National Rugby League. To this day, she says, no-one has proved this isn't true.

Hyphenated-Surname is an avowed monarchist and proud agitator for the return of family values and personal hygiene.

In 2001 she joined a group with other party renegades to protest the Howard Government's treatment of asylum seekers, on the strict proviso that no refugees would be allowed to sit on her furniture.

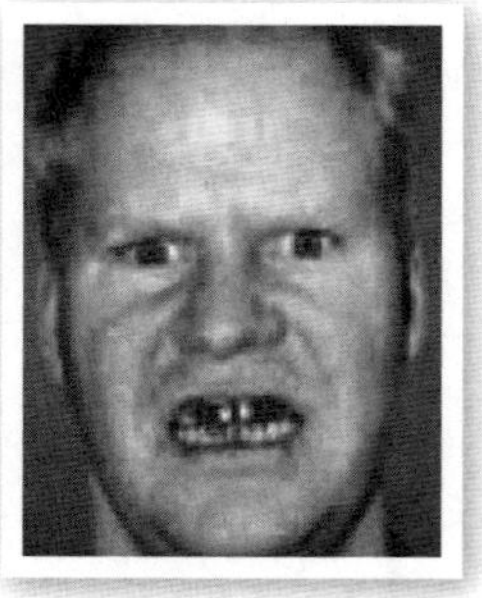

Lester Raincoat

Man of the people, graduate of the university of life with first-class honours

Lester is an Adelaide taxidriver with fifteen years' experience, which has given him a great deal of time to meditate on the problems facing this country.

This remarkable man has now uncovered irrefutable proof that the world is secretly governed by a race of Giant Yellow Lizards. Hillary Clinton? George Bush? Shannon Noll? Giant Lizards. All of them.

In 1998 Lester stood for the thirteenth spot on the One Nation Senate ticket in South Australia. Although, ultimately, he failed to get elected, he has lost none of his enthusiasm for positive civic engagement. These days he is the webmaster for a group of concerned citizens calling itself 'Concerned Citizens Against Everything'.

Karin Gotterdammerung

Conservative blogger and lawyer, former News Ltd columnist

Karin Gotterdammerung has been rolling her eyes and snorting derisively at the 'smelly orthodoxies' of the left ever since she was a child. At the age of five, she successfully brought a High Court injunction against the Department of Education for seeking to admit Muslim children to her kindergarten sandpit. The court accepted her argument that such a move would be an intolerable constraint on her freedom of movement.

Karin came to national attention in 2001 with her article 'Lethal Injections for Junkies a Shot in the Arm for All', a controversial proposal to execute drug addicts in front of small children as part of a 'scared straight' national drug education program.

Gotterdammerung dismissed the ensuing howls of outrage as 'predictable pap from the Howard-haters'.

After her own conviction for possession of cocaine, newspaper editors declined to publish her regular column and her career stalled momentarily. That's when Gotterdammerung hit upon the ingenious idea of connecting with her readers directly by tattooing her work on the stomachs of pigs and hurling the beasts from the back of a ute onto the front lawns of Australian homes.

Her forthcoming book is called *STAB IN THE BACK: Why Lesbian Schoolteachers Want to Kill Your Kids for Al-Qaeda.*

Karin will happily admit that Henry Kissinger once described her as 'hot'!

Bree Tungsten

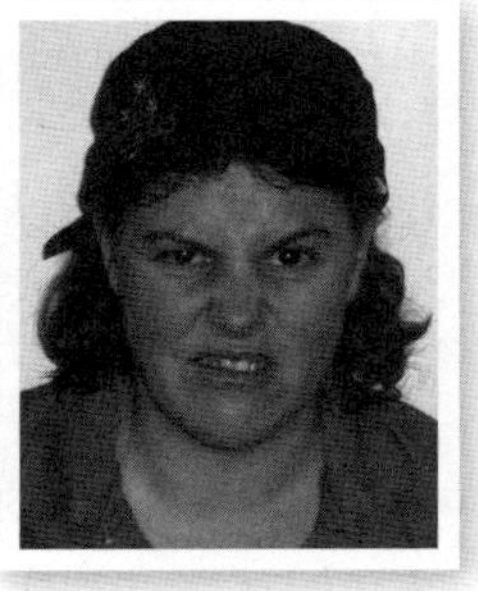

Unionist, social justice activist and friend of all public servants forced to endure inadequate air conditioning

Bree Tungsten is the only remaining member of the Australian Communist Party and shop steward for the CPSU. She knows what it's like to bring the Department of Veterans' Affairs to its knees for its inappropriate use of 'phallocentric' memorial statues.

Tungsten rose to fame during a dispute over a stapler at the Department of Foreign Affairs and Trade, which led to a black ban on the use of all staplers and related office equipment within the Commonwealth Public Service in 1992.

As a result, the federal government was unable to ratify the Convention for the Preservation of Antarctic Seals when a ceiling fan blew the papers out of the window. A jubilant Tungsten claimed it as 'a victory for oppressed seals everywhere'.

Her involvement in this book was made at the insistence of the publishers in order to provide a much needed Marxist-Stalinist-feminist voice. She wishes to make it clear that she does not approve of this book and she's here under sufferance.

How I Came to Meet the Man Called 'Jack the Insider'

by Richard Fidler

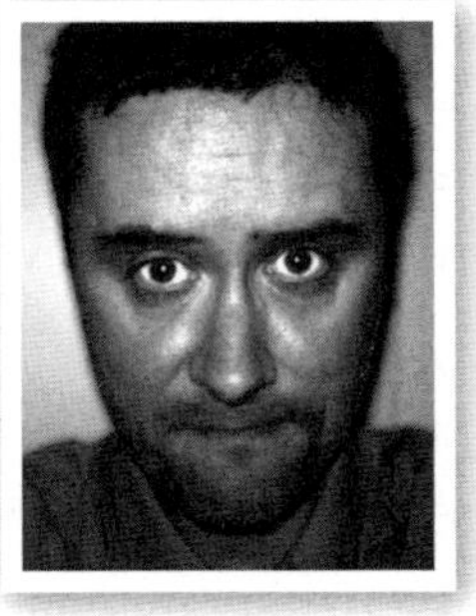

In 1993, I was in Buenos Aires, and caught up in the pleasures of that remarkable city. One evening, after too much Argentinian sparkling wine, I was beaten up and left on the footpath without money or passport.

My problems were compounded by the fact that my visa had expired a few days before. I stumbled into a bar and pushed my last coins into a payphone. The adjutant on duty at the Australian Embassy happened to be an old friend from uni. He told me not to move, and to await the arrival of a highly placed man who could help me, and who just happened to be in the area.

Less than an hour later, the door to the bar swung open and I saw a man, sharply kitted out in a white suit of the kind favoured in the 1950s by US senators on fact-finding missions to Vietnam. His arm was slung around a former prime minister of Australia. The both of them had clearly been enjoying a few schooners of Buenos Aires' finest rioja.

He introduced himself as Jack, and told me he was, for the moment, a Commonwealth public servant. He said I wasn't to worry, he'd sort the whole mess out, but right now, quite frankly, he and the prime minister were parched.

Jack stepped back outside and told the Commonwealth car to wait, while the former PM peeled off a few notes and ordered a round.

In that bar that afternoon I learned more about the way power truly works in Australia than I could from a thousand Paul Kelly books. For instance, did you know that before you become prime minister, you have to let an alien install a remotely controlled grenade inside your head? Well, don't feel too bad, because I didn't know either.

I don't know how Jack sorted my problems out . . . but he did. I have no memory of the intervening hours, but when I came to, I was in business class on an Aeroflot flight to Perth, with a steaming handtowel on my forehead.

I wanted to thank Jack, but I never found out his full name or how to contact him.

A year later, I was in London with friends in an Australian pub, holding my breath, as Juan Antonio Samaranch announced: *and the winner is . . . Syd-er-ney!* While the pub broke out into cheers, I glanced back to the TV and was astonished to see Jack copping a sloppy kiss on both cheeks from a grateful Samaranch.

Then, only last year, I was invited to a fundraiser lunch at the New South Wales State Parliament. Jack was the keynote speaker. He helped himself to some of the parliamentary red and made a passionate speech on behalf of the late former premier Sir Robert Askin.

Jack and a few of his mates from the Upper House enjoy some light refreshment

Afterwards I rushed to his side. He said he remembered me, and then beckoned me through a side door from the dining room that led to a secret tunnel (famously known as 'Max's Back Passage') that had been built in colonial times. We emerged into the inner sanctum of the private members' bar.

There, in that underground cavern, I saw members of parliament, men and women dressed in togas, dancing in circles, burning an effigy of a giant owl. The purpose of this ritual remains mysterious to me even now.

Jack passed me a foaming schooner and confessed he'd been moved to tears by recent demands from our elected leaders that we sign up to some core Australian values and institutions. This was all very well, Jack told me, but how many mug punters have the faintest idea what these things really are, for Christ's sake.

Jack asked for my help. He told me he agreed with Winston Churchill that democracy is the worst form of government in the world, and that the average battler needed to learn the tricks of the trade to nudge it into the right direction to achieve equitable outcomes for the citizen in question.

I was moved by Jack's patriotism and vowed to do what I could to help.

This guide, this tool, this handbook, is the fruit of that afternoon of burning effigies and rampant underground parliamentary fornication. It is, above all, an incitement to action. We place it in your hands …

Jack's Introduction

Why I Wrote This Book

Until now, the history of the civilised world has thrown up only a handful of books worth keeping on your shelves: the *Shorter Oxford Dictionary*, *Roget's Thesaurus*, the *Jacaranda Atlas* and a street map of Kowloon showing the best brothels. (Which isn't really a book, I grant you, but it does come in handy when you're on the go.)

The Insider's Guide to Power in Australia is a seminal text for those who strive to hear the truth about life in Australia.

Australia can be a confusing place, especially for Australians. We have three levels of government; none worth a pinch of shit but all of whom insist you vote for them on a regular basis. We have a corporate world blagging its way around a laughably cobbled together regulatory system while trying not to snigger too much. There's a mutant media that routinely crucifies people, often for no apparent good reason, and a taxation system that, frankly, I gave up on years ago.

It's got so bad that people often pull me up in the street – just out of the blue – grab me by the shoulders and demand to know what's going on. I do my best to tell them but there is so little time to explain it all, especially to those coming down from four-day-long methamphetamine binges.

So in order to avoid any further violence and property crime, I decided to have a crack at explaining how Australia works. In a book, like. I sat down over a few schooners and got it all out, spewing forth wisdom for days on end, disgorging sapience until I uttered my very last word on the subject and collapsed in a pool of urine, faecal matter and ejaculate, all in equal parts. A couple of sheilas did the typing.

I endured this ghastly episode so that, right now, in your trembling hands, you would hold the latchkey to the postern of Australian life – how it works, where you fit in and how you're going to get out of the shit you find yourself in now.

How to Use This Book

The book is written in English and is designed to be read in the traditional left to right manner; commencing at page one and moving along and down and then upwards to the top of page two and continuing thus until you arrive at the last line. At this point a lightly moistened finger will assist in lifting and turning the page to page three, where you begin the process again, and so on.

After You Read This Book

The truth is this book is far more valuable to you than the *Oxford Dictionary* ever could be. Sliding this book alongside an A–Z of the English language and then leaving it there on the shelf will demean it and cast every word I've assembled for your benefit into oblivion. You need to keep it close.

And don't leave it on the bedside table either, to be jumbled in with the wretched refuse of your horrible life: the unopened Bryce Courtenay novel that some cheap idiot bought you, the fetid contraceptive frippery and the stain from the massage oil that left a nasty rash.

Indeed, once you've absorbed its deep, enduring wisdom, I strongly recommend you pop it in a Mylar bag and place it gently in your underpants drawer as a gentle reminder that even if you lose your way and soil yourself again, you can always make a fresh start.

Now get stuck into the book – the lot of youse.

Jack the Insider

CHAPTER ONE

Australia Gets Invented

(Patent Pending)

The History of the Universe and Its Important Role in Creating Australia

The Big Bang and That

Look, before your eyes glaze over, this isn't that bloody hard.

The universe is a tick under 14 billion years old. Well, that's how long it's been since it blew up. No-one from Stephen Hawking down can tell you what was there before the universe blew up. There's a general muttering from all the astrophysicists about density and gravitational singularity but the truth is no-one's quite sure. They do think it was dark. Probably.

The Big Bang: crucial in the invention of Australia

No-one's quite sure why it started when it did either, except to say there's agreement that there were some fairly strong forces at work. There are some God-botherers among your folk in white lab coats who talk about a higher power lighting the wick on the thing, while others babble atheistically about general relativity.

Anyway, the point is, the thing went off in what, clearly, was a pyrotechnically impressive manner about 13.7 billion years ago, give or take a week. When it did, energy levels that would have crushed a lesser universe went through the roof.

But fortunately for all Australians, the universe toughed it out, expanding and cooling while going through various chemical transitions which created matter.

The Creation of Australia

Australia had to wait a further 13.5 billion years to be invented, starting out as a chunk of Gondwanaland on Planet Earth 500 million years ago, wedged up against Africa, South America, the Middle East and Antarctica. Australia very sensibly decided to sever all ties with its neighbours and headed east where there was a lot of space and some very nice beaches.

THE UNSTOPPABLE TIMELINE OF AUSTRALIAN PROGRESS

167 million BC All ties with Antarctica severed

150 million BC Wombats the size of Volkswagens roam the land

40,000 BC Aborigines arrive. Footy possibly invented.

26 January 1788 First Fleet arrives in Sydney Cove

27 January 1788 First post-orgy recovery party

1 January 1901 Australia gets invented

1914 Australia is cordially invited to attend World War I

1929 Australia is forced to endure the Great Depression without Jeff Kennett's beyondblue

1930 Don Bradman invents batting

1931 Phar Lap on the gear in the US

1932 Phar Lap dead

1939 World War II: Australia is slow to declare war as Prime Minister Menzies is unsure whether to fight with or against the Japanese

1941 Alan Jones born, gives mother stern lecture on breastfeeding

1972 Brockie invents motor racing

1969 First Holden V8 built

One hundred and fifty million years and a few earthquakes later, Australia had settled down to become what it is today: the biggest South Pacific island resort on the market.

The First Australians

People back then used to walk a lot more than we do now. And so it seems the first Australians wandered over from South-East Asia. They may even have walked all the way from Africa. Which is a bloody long way. Or perhaps they just paddled in canoes from the Straits of Mallaca. However they managed it, at some point they caught a glimpse of the jewel in the sea and thought, 'Yes, this'll do nicely.'

The first Australians eschewed farming after failed attempts to herd wombats, but they learned to get a feed out of the place, even in the most desolate deserts on earth.

They set fire to a lot of Australia. No-one knows whether they did so in sadness or in anger. They brought their dogs with them. They may have invented footy.

'What a Fucking Terrible Place for a Country'

About 40,000 years later, a Dutchman, Willem Janszoon, sailed south of Papua New Guinea aboard the ship *Duyfken*, lobbing on Cape York Peninsula in 1606.

Believed to be the first European to set foot on Australian soil, Janszoon looked about and declared, 'What a fucking terrible place for a country', promptly pulled up anchor and sailed off.

In what may have been the biggest real estate debacle of all time, another Dutchman, Abel Tasman, circumnavigated Australia without actually seeing any of it – with the exception of a bit of southern Tasmania, which he mistook for something else. He headed off to New Zealand and then sailed back to Malaysia, never again setting eyes on Australian soil. Returning to his master, Anthony Van Diemen, the governor-general of the Dutch East Indies, Tasman reported, 'If Australia's out there, I'll be buggered if I can find it.'

The British, always quick to leap on an opportunity, figured they'd sail up and down the southern oceans looking for

Terra Australis Incognita until they banged into something that seemed to fit the general description. When someone did bang into it, that someone was Captain James Cook aboard the *Endeavour* and that something turned out to be Botany Bay.

Cook liked what he saw so much he stuck a Union Jack in the sand and declared, 'I hereby proclaim this country in the name of whatever demented, syphilitic madman currently straddles the throne of England.'

Captain Cook: his role in the invention of Australia has always been overrated

THE UNSTOPPABLE TIMELINE OF AUSTRALIAN PROGRESS

1972 Whitlam Government elected on a platform of invigorating Australian culture

1975 Whitlam Government cast out in record landslide defeat

1977 Kerry Packer invents cricket

1977 Sir John Kerr gets shit-faced at the Melbourne Cup

1979 Roger Rogerson awarded a medal for services to police superannuation

1983 Potato farmer Cliff Young runs from Sydney to Melbourne in a pair of gumboots. To this day, no-one knows why.

1984 Jack is NOT involved in the Fine Cotton Ring-In

1986 Malcolm Fraser gets dacked in Memphis

1991 Shane Warne invents bowling

1996 Australians hand in their firearms in the gun buy-back scheme, ensuring guns remain in the hands of criminals where they belong

2000 Sydney hosts a party that is gatecrashed by troublemakers from around the world. Fortunately, most of them go home when the city runs out of beer.

2002 The cane toad population hits 200 million

2006 Steve 'The Stingray Guy' Irwin dies while performing at a petting zoo for funnel-web spiders

The locals, keeping a lookout, replied, 'Oh, a country. Is that what it is? And here's us thinking we're living in an existential vortex.' The British, who tend not to handle sarcasm well, started shooting.

A Top Spot for a Prison

The Brits were astonished by the beauty of the landscape and immediately set Australia up as a prison. Convicted criminals were dispatched to Australia to build the Cahill Expressway, fast-food outlets and gigantic plastic fruits along the eastern seaboard. Many of their heartbreaking travails were captured on video and got a run on *Australia's Funniest Home Videos.* A great nation was born.

Happily for all students of the caper, Australian history is a doddle to grasp and therefore little time need be wasted acquainting oneself with it. Walter Lindrum, Phar Lap and the Don – that's all you'll ever really need to know about Australian history and everyone knows the history there, right? The Don got a blob in his last knock, Phar Lap was given a hot shot, and Walter Lindrum was hounded out of his sport by the rule makers of an arcane parlour game, too fucking up themselves to realise greatness when they saw it.

The Job's Done

The important thing to note is that right from the Big Bang, all that fuss was just a lead-up to this one moment in time and this one particular spot in the universe: Australia in the twenty-first century.

If your eyes are getting a bit weepy and your knees are trembling right now, well that's only fit and proper. All the work's been done. Australia has been served up to you on a plate: you might as well stick your face in and suck the succulent morsels right up your nostrils.

The Constitution and That

The legal business of inventing Australia was long, incredibly boring and nothing you really need to bother yourself with. Except for this...

Australia got invented in an alcoholic haze by some of the worst people in the country. The so-called National Australasian Constitutional Convention was held in Sydney in 1891.

As you can see by the convention's title, they were all so thoroughly pissed they couldn't even spell 'Australian' properly.

Nowadays, there's much made of Australia's Federation – bloated mythology most of it. I'm here to tell you that it was a long and boring process run by some of the nation's greatest philanderers and no-hopers.

In 1889, Sir Henry Parkes arranged a bit of a constitutional convention at the New South Wales Parliament to get the federation ball rolling. A lot of Australia's finest legal and political minds turned up and got as drunk as monkeys for the entire two days.

Sir Henry Parkes spoke to the inebriated throng on the first day, albeit briefly:

THE NATIONAL AUSTRALASIAN CONSTITUTIONAL CONVENTION
Sydney, March 1891

DAY ONE

8.15 am	Introduction – Welcome
8.20 am	Light Refreshment
11.45 am	Keynote Address by Alfred Deakin *'We meet here today with the eyes of the world upon us. It is our responsibility to have a few drinks, pop off to the races and – time permitting – have a chat about inventing Australia.'*
11.48 am	Light Refreshment
2.12 pm	Lunch
8.45 pm	Workshop – *How to Ban Aborigines from Joining the Australian Natives Association*
8.49 pm	Dinner & Light Refreshment

DAY TWO

Rest Day

DAY THREE

8.15 am	Light Refreshment
3.30 pm	Honesty Session – *Who Put the Turd in Alfred Deakin's Shoe Last Night?*
4.15 pm	Police Summoned
4.45 pm	Light Refreshment
12.00 pm	Conference Closes

The Agenda for the Sydney Constitutional Convention: Parkes hijacked the show, behaved disgracefully and got almost as drunk as I am right now

Welcome to Henry Parkes's Australia of the future.
Who here among you is not sick to death of having to pass
through customs every time we cross state borders in this wide, brown land?

There was a general distracted murmur and the clink of glasses, which Parkes took as a sign to continue. He regaled everyone with a gruesome anecdote of his latest encounter with customs in Wodonga, where Victorian authorities conducted a body cavity search on the old bugger, turning up some wrought-iron outdoor furniture and a pound of grapes.

Parkes finished his oratory by seeking leave so he could get on with the important business of buggering delegates' wives.

Later that night, he returned to the conference and was heard saying: 'Fuck Australia. Get me another schooner.'

A melee ensued thereafter: a good, old-fashioned donnybrook. Struggling poet and journalist Henry Lawson jumped in after Parkes put the hard word on Mary Gilmore, the love of Lawson's life.

Henry Lawson almost lost an eye at the Sydney Convention

She was a good sort, Mary, and I don't mind admitting that I get as hard as a cat's head whenever I look at a tenner.

Anyway, Henry demanded that Parkes apologise and got glassed for his trouble. When Henry regained his composure, he remarked that blood had stained the bottle, a line he has been misquoted on to this day.

Parkes's appalling behaviour at the Sydney Convention set Federation back four years, until someone got the bright idea of having another convention; this time leaving the old bastard off the invitation list, so they could get on and invent Australia without any more distractions.

The Corowa Conference, 1893

Why everyone had to go to Corowa, a backwater not fit for man or beast, is a mystery. My own guess is that they figured if they held the delegates hostage for long enough, they'd agree to anything just to get out of the place and go home.

Most historians love to focus on the 'official' deliberations of the conference itself. The truth is that the real action was at the Royal Hotel in downtown Corowa.

On the opening night Alfred Deakin held court in the front bar. Even then he was a threepenny pissant, angling to have a university named after him. But he was a very big drinker in those days and quick with a shout, so he had his uses.

Alfred Deakin: a great leader. He led the way at the Corowa Convention. To the bar, to the golf course, to the races and then back to the bar again.

One delegate expressed the frustrations of many, shouting at Deakin: 'I hope this isn't another waste of time. It's taken me twelve hours to get here. The public transport in this country is a fucking disgrace.'

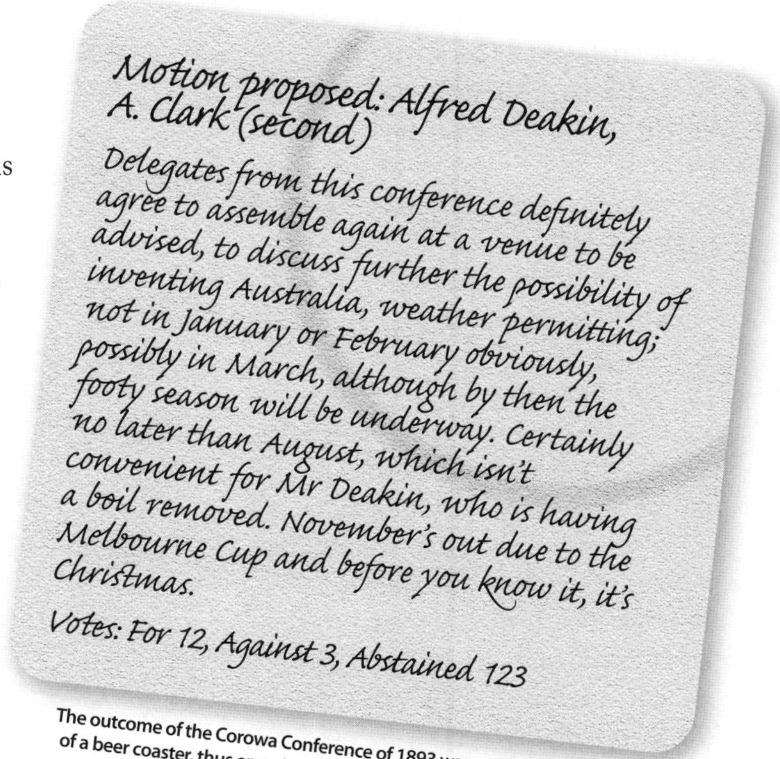
Motion proposed: Alfred Deakin, A. Clark (second)

Delegates from this conference definitely agree to assemble again at a venue to be advised, to discuss further the possibility of inventing Australia, weather permitting; not in January or February obviously, possibly in March, although by then the footy season will be underway. Certainly no later than August, which isn't convenient for Mr Deakin, who is having a boil removed. November's out due to the Melbourne Cup and before you know it, it's Christmas.

Votes: For 12, Against 3, Abstained 123

The outcome of the Corowa Conference of 1893 was scrawled down on the back of a beer coaster, thus ensuring it was preserved in perpetuity for all Australians

Deakin assured him that the conference was the real deal and that Parkes would not be in attendance as he had been hurled into a gibbet by his many creditors. New South Wales politician George Reid was smoking opium in a Sydney brothel and that troublemaker, Edmund 'Toby Toss-Pot' Barton, had bought himself a new mirror and would be masturbating feverishly over his reflection for the foreseeable.

One of the Tasmanian delegates, Andrew Inglis Clark, was sitting in the corner of the Royal Hotel, writing a draft of the Australian Constitution on the back of a beer coaster. He'd gotten as far as scrawling 'No Poofters' before he hit a bit of a hurdle on the separation of powers. He was drinking heavily and coughing up phlegm into a spittoon for consumptives.

These blokes managed to cobble the Federation together, but it was a botched job. Many delegates left in disgust. They just couldn't come at the idea of Western Australia being part of a federated Australia and I can't either. Bunch of bloody blow-ins, the lot of them. They didn't deserve to get a guernsey in a federated Australia. They didn't deserve it then and they don't deserve it now.

Australia had to get its act together, knock out a constitution, invent a few political parties, hire an army and some federal wallopers before it could hang out the shingle to the rest of the world. The clock was ticking and Australia knew time was running out. Australia did what it would subsequently do on numerous occasions when faced with almost insurmountable challenges: wing it.

The drinks bill at the Corowa Convention came to a staggering £4 million. Deakin did a runner, so the publican forwarded the bill to the New South Wales Government. NSW Premier Parkes refused to pay the tab and, as a result, the country was plunged into the depression of 1890–1891.

Papering over the Cracks in Australian Democracy

When you think of the constitution, think of it as being a bit like your dear old nanna – a relic from the horse and buggy era who hates any kind of change and is deeply uncomfortable around blackfellas.

The constitution sets out the basis of our whole system of government. In fact the government would be illegal without it and would probably be stuck in prison, offering sexual favours for packets of smokes. Cynics will tell you that our constitution isn't worth the paper it's written on, but that's just bullshit. I know this for a fact. Back in the mid eighties, Hawkie used it to wipe up our drinks slops after we'd had a big night on the piss at the Lodge. He held up the dripping document and asked me to 'do something with it', then promptly forgot all about it.

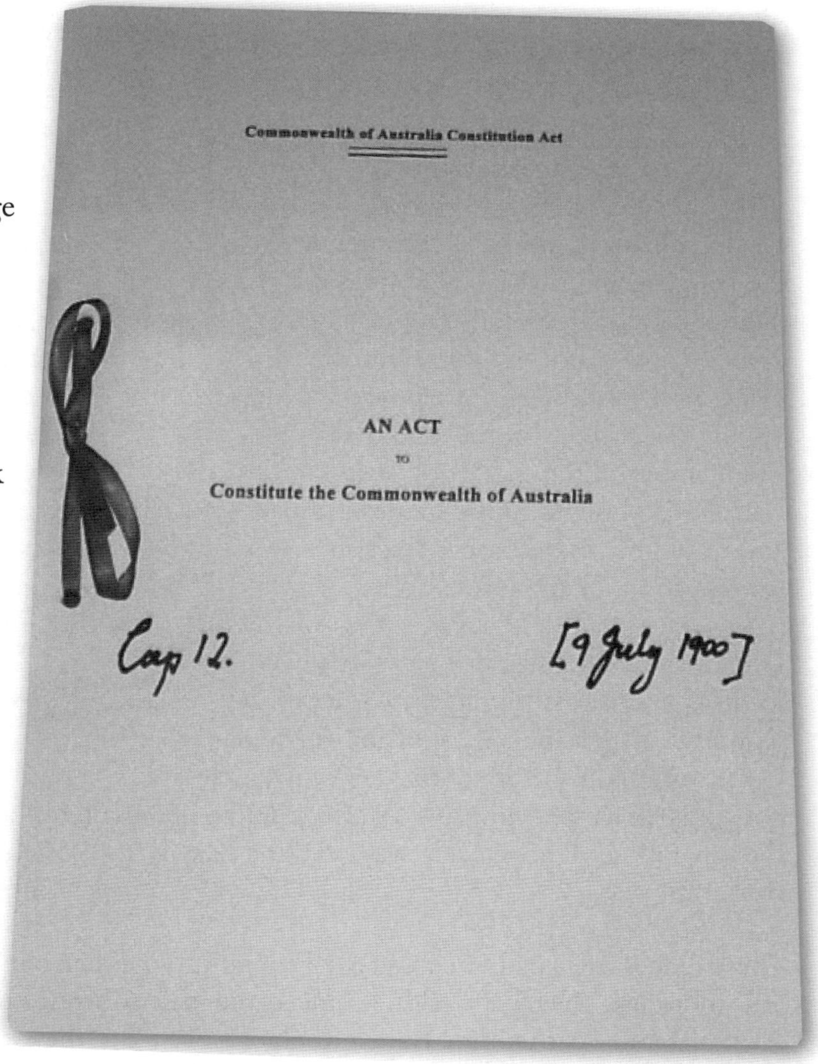

The constitution: tied up with a girlish ribbon

Despite the water damage, a couple of dealers in rare manuscripts quoted me some figures, all of them in the $150–$250 range, which is clearly a lot more than the $1.25 you'd pay to pick up the same value in blank stationery at Officeworks . . . proving the nay-sayers wrong. But I couldn't be arsed driving to IKEA to pick up a decorative frame for the damn thing so I quietly returned it to the National Library on a no-questions-asked basis.

But I did have a chance to study our nation's founding document. And even with the beer goggles on it didn't take me long to realise the enormity of the thing that our Founding Fathers had wrought.

Like most legal documents, the constitution begins by stating the bleeding obvious at great length:

> 'The Commonwealth' shall mean the Commonwealth of Australia as established under this Act.
> 'The States' shall mean such of the colonies of New South Wales, New Zealand, Queensland, Tasmania, Victoria, Western Australia, and South Australia . . .

Did you spot that?

'The States' shall mean such of the colonies of New South Wales, New Zealand . . .

It's titbits like that that lead any serious student of constitutional law to ask: were our Founding Fathers on drugs? Imagine the chaos and horror if New Zealand was incorporated into Australia as a state. Kiwis would all come over here, go on the dole and clog up our beaches, and we couldn't let that happen to Australia, could we?

Queen Victoria assumed absolute control of Australia before getting stuck in to create the preconditions for World War I

Sovereignty: You're Not the Boss of Me

The first question that our Founding Fathers had to figure out was this: where does all legitimate sovereign power in Australia really lie? A few tried to argue that it lay with the Australian people, but ultimately it was decided to invest all sovereign power in a small, unpleasant woman who lived in England and had a nasty bladder problem.

And so it is to this day. Supreme power rests within the body of the Queen and then the golden stream of power trickles down her leg to her representative in Australia: the governor-general. The GG has it for half a second before it's snatched away by the prime minister, who then tells the rest of us to sit down, shut up and do as we're told.

But the constitution doesn't even mention the prime minister; it hands supreme power to the governor-general, stipulating that office bearers under the Crown should be dressed as playing cards. Reading the constitution is a bit like dating a girl who went to a private school . . . it's all about what's not being said. That's why we need . . .

Conventions: The Raw, Bleeding Meat of Australian Democracy

It's often said that the constitution is just the bare bones of our parliamentary system. The so-called conventions are the flesh and blood that give it life.

Conventions are unwritten laws that everyone has to obey, except for those in the Liberal Party, who are given a special 'opt-out' provision if the convention in question turns out to be too boring.

Confused? Let me give you some examples of these unwritten laws.

Mandy Vandy hard at work for her employer, the Australian taxpayer

Ministers are responsible for their departments
This principle held firm for decades, until Amanda Vanstone was craned into the Department of Immigration and Multicultural Affairs. Despite presiding over obscene levels of incompetence, Mandy Vandy refused to resign, shrewdly realising that when you violate an 'unwritten law' no-one's actually going to arrest you. Eventually she was sacked by John Howard for eating one of her staffers.

If a minister misleads the parliament, the minister must resign
That's a bit hilarious these days, isn't it?

Saddam Hussein has weapons of mass destruction.
Iraq: mission accomplished!
The economy has turned the corner.

Ministers have since realised they can ethically squirm out of these tricky situations with the 'only joking' defence.

If a senator dies or resigns, a nominee from the same party is appointed to replace him or her
The Coalition parties overturned this convention in 1975 so they could stack the Senate and stop the Whitlam Government from building a giant pipeline across the country out of Lego. Once in office, the Liberals quickly reinstated the convention in the form of a constitutional amendment. This was thought necessary to discourage senators from assassinating each other in the chamber.

The Parliament: A Bunch of Upright Members

Like many other enlightened countries, Australia has a **bicameral** parliament. Not one legislative chamber, but two: the **House of Representatives** and the **Senate**.

Experts often liken the place to a Qantas 767. The House of Reps is like economy, and the Senate is like business class – there are fewer seats and the general tone of the place is better, but ultimately it's up to the economy section to physically overpower the pilot and take over the plane.

The House of Reps is where governments are formed and the big issues of the day are debated. You and your neighbours elect your local member, who either lives nearby or will reluctantly agree to commute to your shitty electorate from Mosman or Kew.

In 1986, maverick senator Mal Colston broke the world Tim Tam eating record by knocking back 148 of the chocolate wafer biscuits in ninety seconds. Mal's secret? He smeared the biscuits in lard so they'd slide more easily through his alimentary canal.

Senators are supposed to take a broader view. They're elected to represent everyone in their state, which means, in effect, that they represent no-one – besides the factional idiots who got them preselected, that is.

The government sponsors most legislation. If a bill is to become law it must pass a vote in the House and then a vote in the Senate, where it can sometimes be defeated. In fact the Senate even has the power to block the government's money supply, making it the most powerful upper house in the world. Which is why people always say to me . . .

Westminster . . . or Washminster????!!!

The Founding Fathers agonised whether we should go for the Westminster system or the US-style presidential system. For a while delegates toyed with the 'Ottoman Empire system', whereby Australia would be ruled by an all-powerful sultan, living in a perfumed, fragrant palace, his body shaved and oiled by a thousand-strong harem every day, but Parkes was quickly voted down. He was never the same after that.

Even so, the constitution is still kind of sexy. Think of it as a greatest hits album of the hottest political systems of the nineteenth century. It cleverly takes the best of the Westminster system from the UK to provide the sturdy central framework, and then it tacks on a bit of the United States as well, like a henhouse on the side.

That's why experts to this day insist it isn't so much a Westminster system as it is a *Washminster* system. It's cheeky puns like these that can keep a conference of political scientists chuckling for hours.

The Senate: Unrepresentative Swill – But Still Somehow Tasty

So while our House of Representatives is based on the British House of Commons, our 'upper house' is similar to the United States Senate. This was deemed necessary for three reasons:

1. Australia couldn't have a house of lords as we have no aristocracy.
2. Just like the US, some kind of states' house was needed as a check against an overly powerful federal government.
3. The Founding Fathers thought that a senate would be like a kind of really cool, sexy, all-night legislative toga party.

Every prime minister in the autumn of his administration will at some point look out into the dark Canberra night and wail: *Why the fuck do we need a senate anyway?*

It's a very good question. And for an answer we must look to the Americans, who also grappled with this very issue as they founded their great republic. In 1780, Thomas Jefferson famously asked George Washington why America would need a senate, given that it already had a house of representatives.

Washington grinned slyly, pulled his breeches from the crack of his bum and asked Jefferson in return, 'Why do you pour your coffee into the saucer before you drink it?'

Jefferson replied, 'None of your business, you pox-addled slave-monger, but since you asked, it is to cool the coffee before I drink it.'

The Senate and the House of Reps: Australia's bicameral legislature ensures Australia is constantly at war with itself

'Just so,' said Washington. 'The Senate will allow time for any legislation conceived in the heat of passion to cool, and to be soberly considered, unlike the small army of bastard children you fathered with your slaves, you priapic hypocrite.'

Thus a high and lofty principle was born. And Australia's Founding Fathers said: *We'll have some of that too.* And aside from a near bout of civil war in 1975, it's worked a treat ever since.

The House of Representatives: Animal Farm or People's House?

The House proudly calls itself 'The People's House', as a reminder of its strong democratic virtues. North Korea calls itself the 'Democratic Peoples' Republic of Korea' for exactly the same reason.

The Founding Fathers envisaged a house that would bring all the disparate elements of the nation together under one roof, giving them all an equal say.

Any visitor to the public gallery of the House of Reps is immediately taken by the range and depth of humanity on display in the bearpit below. They come to Canberra from the inner cities, the outer suburbs, the bush, the coasts, the dry inland areas, the farms, the tropics and the snow. And just as the Founding Fathers intended, the astonishing diversity of these regions is reflected in our parliamentarians, leading the Australian Bureau of Statistics to conclude that 48% of all Australians are lawyers; 56% are former political staffers; 62% are former presidents of a university chocolate appreciation society; and 78% of all Australians are men, most of them with several angry ex-wives.

The Prime Minister: A Freak of Nature?

One of Australia's most endearing quirks is that every single one of our prime ministers has been a middle-aged or elderly white male.

Mathematicians often ponder this bizarre statistical anomaly, and liken the odds to rolling a six forty times in a row. Over the decades this has settled into a fun Australian tradition; indeed the 100 per cent middle-aged white guy success rate has become an object of whimsical national affection, like mateship and the Big Pineapple. Here's hoping that feral bloodnut Julia Gillard has the decency to put her leadership ambitions on hold so we can maintain this beloved institution.

The weirdest thing about the prime minister is that he doesn't exist. The PM is mentioned nowhere in the constitution. Nowhere. He is recognised only under the broader grouping of 'ministers of the crown', so his status as head of government is legally very shaky, to say the least.

It makes me wonder. We've had plenty of big, ugly and ambitious treasurers in recent decades; I cannot for the life of me understand why the treasurer doesn't simply enter the cabinet room, give the PM a bit of a thump, slide into his seat and insist that he'll be chairing the meeting from now on. Keating was bigger and nastier than Hawkie. Costello? Much bigger than Little Johnnie (although admittedly not as nasty).

All that power, and everything that comes with it – the jet, the house, the wine cellar, the grovelling underlings, the lot – rests entirely on a name that isn't even recognised in the constitution! The treasurer should just announce he's head of government, and the prime minister is now the minister in charge of . . . prime numbers or something. I don't know.

No Change! For the Sake of No Change!

Although it's a piece of piss to overturn a convention, it's not so easy to change the black letter law of the constitution itself.

The constitution was designed to stand the test of time, to withstand the clamour of crazy, impulsive, ideological fashions of the day. Think of it as a grand old gent in a classic blazer, cravat and cream slacks. And you want to put him in a puff jacket and low-slung hipster jeans that show his arse-crack? I don't think so, my friend.

That's why the Founding Fathers set the bar on constitutional change very high. Section 128 says that any changes must be put to a national vote and approved by a majority of people in a majority of states. That means that five people in Tasmania, Queensland and Western Australia can thwart the will of the nation.

Australians have had forty-two opportunities to change their constitution, and only eight attempts have been successful. It doesn't matter how good the idea is: all it takes is for the Broncos to lose a match or for Ricky Ponting to make a blob and the whole thing goes down in flames. Cop that Australia!

Australian Democracy: A Dissenting View

Most people think Australia is a 'democracy'. That we're run by elected officials who do our bidding, eh?

Nothing could be further from the truth, my friend.

After years of thinking about Australia and its problems, quietly meditating in my cab, I've come to understand that this country is run by a cabal of Giant Yellow Lizards. It has been since the year dot.

Peter Costello. Julia Gillard. Shannon Noll. Giant Lizards. The lot of them.

And the beauty of it is that they need not wear any disguise: people expect to see a human when they look at these Eight-Foot Yellow Lizards . . . so that's what they see. When I realised that I nearly shat my tracky daks, ay.

This is not a democracy because no matter who you vote for, a Lizard always gets in. I once confronted Peter Costello about this when he got in my cab, and the bastard agreed with me. Can you fucken believe that? He knows I know that we know and he doesn't care.

The Giant Lizards are taking over and there's not much anyone can do to stop it. If you want to live, do what I do: I'm collecting millions of dead flies in my empty rainwater tank at home. When the Lizards come for me, I just hope they accept it as an offering and they don't hatch their babies in my abdomen.

The GG and Me

It's a long story and I'm reluctant to tell it here but I attended my last day at the races at the Melbourne Cup in 1977, with the then governor-general, Sir John Kerr. Now, I was never a fan of his, what with him toadying up to the Windsors all the time. And in that top hat and tails he looked like a complete goose.

But he was a very, very big drinker and quick with a shout, so I joined him at the Members' Bar on that fateful day. We were getting stuck into schooners of cream sherry. Now Kerr was a sherry man – he was mad for the cream sherry. It's the vice-regal drink of choice of course, but he didn't realise I'd spent a lot of time in Spain propping up Generalissimo Franco's regime in the 1960s, and I'd developed a real taste for the stuff. Long story short, by the time the winner, Gold and Black, saluted at the leger, poor old Johnnie Kerr was a blithering heap.

There were 90,000 people there that day, all of them drunk as monkeys, so I don't know why the Victorian Racing Club picked on Kerr and me. But they did. And they barred us for life for public drunkenness. I mean, I was fine, but Kerr was a real mess. He had vomit all down the front of him and had soiled his trousers during the presentation of the cup. He got a bit confused too, while making his speech on the podium – kissing a startled Bart Cummings hard on the lips, slapping the owner's wife on the backside and asking the 42-year-old winning jockey, little Johnnie Duggan, where he went to school.

I thought everyone would take it in good humour. But Kerr didn't have many mates by then and when the stewards pulled him up and took him down to the stables, he was mucked out with a hose and a big soapy brush before they sent us on our way.

It was very undignified for a man of his position. He had to clamber into the vice-regal roller in his underpants. And we've never been back – barred for life, as I say. Of course Sir John Kerr dropped off the branch a few years later, so it didn't cost him much, but I've suffered for his indiscretions for nigh on thirty years. And what did I do to deserve that, eh? All I did was enjoy a few schooners with a mate, had a punt and took a few dollars off the bookies.

Oh, and the Fine Cotton Ring-In. But I wouldn't know anything about that.

One more for the road? Kerr demands a schooner of cream sherry on that terrible day.

How Power Works in Australia: The Official Version

It's a little known fact that Australian democracy was designed according to ancient Hindu principles: power trickles down through the various chakras of the body politic, getting filthier the further it goes down. This is how it's supposed to work . . .

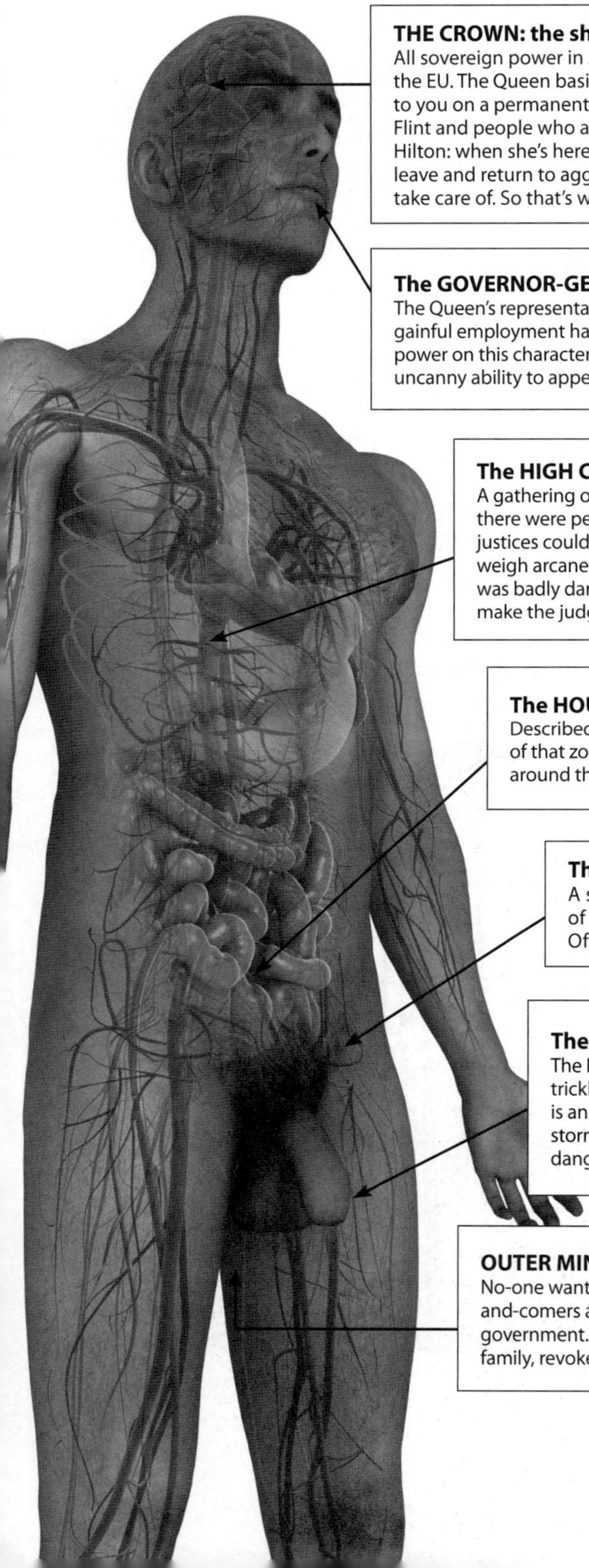

THE CROWN: the shiny brain clamp of our heritage
All sovereign power in Australia lies with an obscure monarch living in a gastronomically challenged nation in the EU. The Queen basically owns your colonial arse. The good news is that she gives control of your life back to you on a permanent loan basis. It's this kind of generosity that has won her the undying allegiance of David Flint and people who are exactly like him. Sadly, Queenie can't be here all the time for us. She's a lot like Paris Hilton: when she's here we love her, she has a great time, she does some ecstasy. But after a while she has to leave and return to aggressively promoting Britain's trade interests ahead of our own. She's got other shit to take care of. So that's why she needs . . .

The GOVERNOR-GENERAL: the open, gaping mouth of protection
The Queen's representative in Australia is the governor-general. The GG is usually a harmless idiot whose lack of gainful employment has become an embarrassment to everyone. Our constitution confers a huge amount of power on this character but in reality he has to do as he's told. The successful applicant will have great hair and an uncanny ability to appear fascinated while stumbling through a découpage exhibition in rural Queensland.

The HIGH COURT: the trembling backbone of the constitution
A gathering of the nation's finest legal minds, the High Court took just ninety-one years to realise that there were people living here before white settlement. Sworn to uphold the constitution, the seven justices could be a real thorn in the side of a government if they wanted to, but most appear content to weigh arcane legal matters of little or no import and work on their novels at night. The court's prestige was badly damaged in 2004 by comments from a *Big Brother* housemate that those big, horsey wigs make the judges look 'kind of gay'. Contrary to popular belief, Kyle Sandilands does not sit on this court.

The HOUSE OF REPRESENTATIVES: the bowel system of democracy
Described optimistically as the 'People's House', it's easily the most horrible place in the world. Think of that zoo enclosure where you saw a gorilla drop faecal matter into its hand and then fling it around the cage. Its members are all single parents, or will be in five years' time.

The SENATE: the urinary tract of legislation
A states' house that votes along party lines. This is a soberer chamber than the House of Reps; 'sober' in the sense that senators shout a lot less but drink a whole lot more. Often alone.

The PRIME MINISTER and CABINET: the blood-engorged genitals of authority
The PM is the only genuinely powerful character in this misleading diagram. Power trickles down and forms a deep murky pool for him to splash around in. In theory, the PM is answerable to parliament, but that's like saying that Darth Vader is answerable to his stormtroopers. The Cabinet gets its name from a former prime minister who accumulated dangerous amounts of power by appointing bits of furniture to the key ministerial positions.

OUTER MINISTRY: the tender perineum of desire
No-one wants to be here. A hellish region of executive government, populated by ambitious up-and-comers and duds from the National Party or former trade union hacks, depending on who's in government. On no account should you tease them about their lowly status: they will set fire to your family, revoke your citizenship and dump you in a Filipino orphanage.

How Power Really Works in Australia

The truth is a lot more complicated. As you can see, political power in Australia devolves from Australia's sweetheart, Bindi Irwin, then passes through a careful filtration process before it arrives on your TV screen in the form of a Sky News poll. But don't worry. The persons named below are all wonderful human beings.

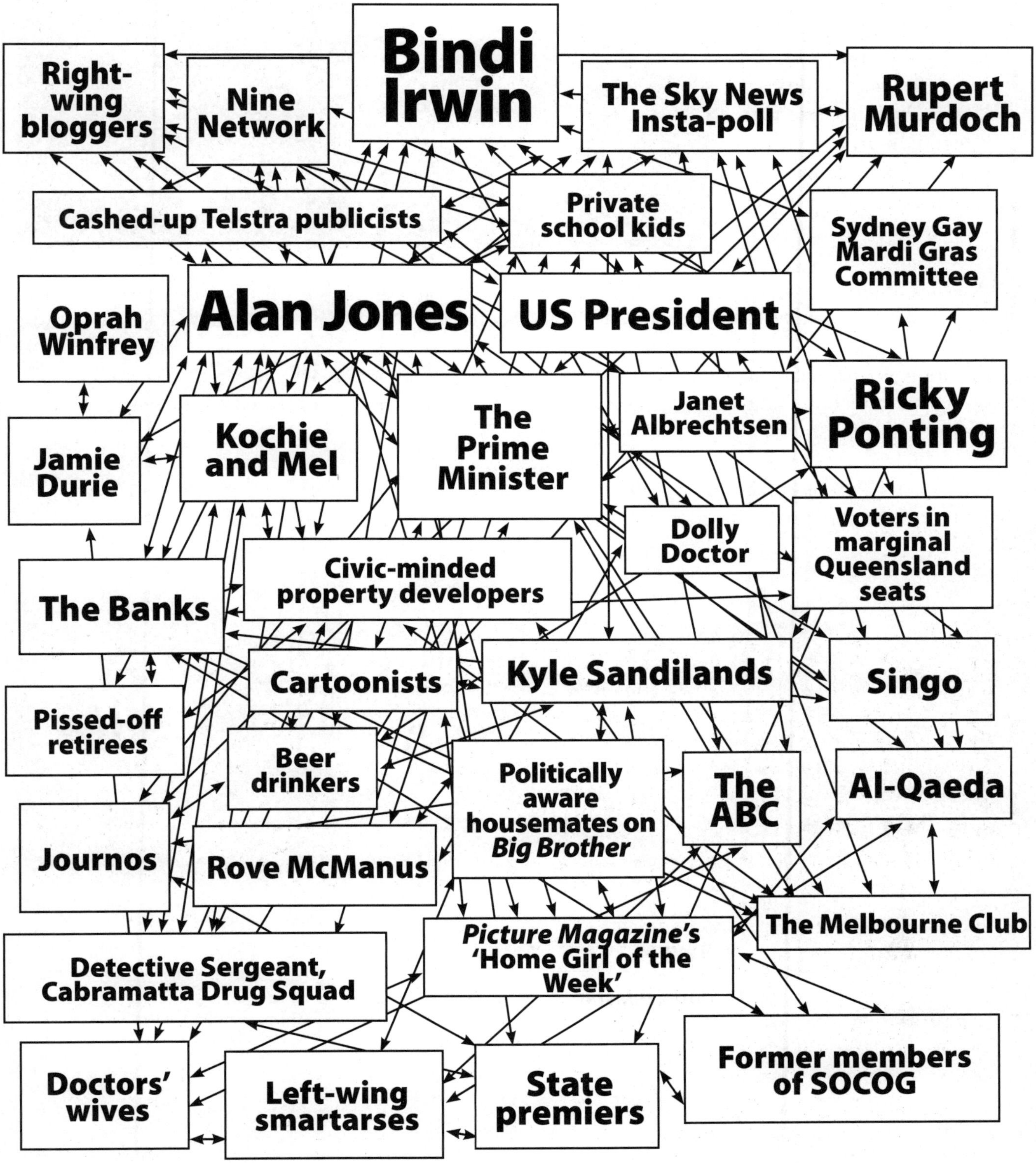

Symbols of Australianness

The Flag

Australia's flag was chosen in 1901 after a worldwide competition was held to find a design that would flutter in the heart of a proud new nation. As no entries were received, Alfred Deakin scratched out a quick drawing on the back of a beer coaster and flung it at a seamstress.

Deakin's rough sketch featured an array of iconic Australian images: meat pies, footballs, kangaroos and Holden cars spread around the playing surface of the Melbourne Cricket Ground.

The original Australian flag came back from the shop with the Union Jack roughly sewn into the top right-hand corner and a handful of glitter stuck to the surface. Deakin accepted the new flag but refused to pay for it.

I dunno, it's kind of grown on me. And it's not as if we can get rid of it. Then what would bloated semi-naked men wear to the cricket?

POINTS TAKEN – CHIF STIFFS THE FLAG

The five largest stars on the Australian flag have seven points while the smallest star has only five. The two points were removed from the smallest star at the insistence of Prime Minister Ben Chifley as part of a post-war austerity drive. Maritime unions reacted angrily, commencing industrial action on the docks which lasted more than half a century.

The Tragedy of Our Flag

14 July 1996: Sunday evening. A barren time. Everything's fucked. Howard leers at us triumphantly on the evening news. Hanson storms the country and funding for my screenplay of *The Tree* (the story of the growth of the Tree of Knowledge in Barcaldine from a sapling to a mighty eucalyptus, to be filmed in real time) has at last been rejected by the AFC. And so the film was never made. And the tree was never properly cherished and protected. And the tree was in due course poisoned by some drunken Young Liberals. But I digress, I digress . . .

Gough and I were sharing a bottle of port in front of his fireplace. The great man looked momentarily bereft. He leaned across and whispered mournfully, 'Comrade, a little more port, if I may.'

His meaning was clear. He seemed to be saying that his life's work had been eroded in the flood tide of conservative mean-spiritedness. I brushed the flecks of cheese from my tie and said, 'It's all the fault of the flag, you know.'

Gough arched his eyebrows and noisily passed wind. I had his attention.

'Gough, it's a joke and you know that better than anyone. It's got the Union Jack in the corner. Inside the Union Jack are the flags of St George, St Andrew and Patrick as well. Our flag is a flag inside a flag inside a flag. Nothing much good can come from a nation with a flag like a fucking Russian doll, Gough.'

Gough, mistaking the family cat for the soda siphon, clutched its neck and squeezed it, testily. He was angry because he knew I was right. Again.

'Now comrade, you've had that bottle to yourself for a good while now . . .'

I smiled and recalled another shared evening, twenty-one years earlier: a fondue party at the Lodge. Both of us much younger and our heads swimming with the sublime delusions of youth. On that festive evening (*Bliss was it in that dawn to be alive/But to be young was very heaven . . .*) I withdrew into a corner with a pen and a bottle of Gough's best single malt. I was hastily scrawling something on a paper napkin when I sensed his towering presence. 'What have you got there, comrade?'

I met his gaze directly and handed him the napkin.

'It's a new flag, Gough. A flag that gives clear moral instruction to the nation . . . an image that says we've come of age.'

My design was simple: the image of Malcolm Fraser, crossed out, with the words LIBS FUCK OFF AND DIE boldly stencilled across it. Gough smiled and wordlessly pocketed the napkin and retrieved his scotch. I took this as an assurance that he would put it to caucus the next day.

But Gough had other priorities. And so the flag was never changed. And the nation was never galvanised to its image and its values. And Gough was never strengthened in his fight to overcome the Tories and was sacked. And he never completed his term in office, and everything we held dear was lost forever.

And so it was. And so it is. And so it goes . . .

Your Filthy Vegan Child Just Threw up on My Flag

On Sunday, while hurling darts at anti-war demonstrators from the eighth floor of the Citibank building, I noticed the absurd image of a dirty, bong-addled slacker and his vegan trollop stumbling through the streets, chanting their mad, anarchic slogans. The trollop held the product of their filthy sexual congress to her breast. Dressed in a batik nappy, the mewling urchin clutched an Australian flag in her hands.

It was one of those 'What's wrong with this picture?' moments. Amid all the symbols of political anachronism and moral nihilism, here was an innocent child trying to make a statement: a single, solitary voice of reason. Or so it seemed.

As the chants for Bush's impeachment and Howard's summary execution reached a fever pitch, the child smiled and then vomited on the flag. The crowd cheered as the puke dripped from the symbol of our nationhood.

Little more than eighteen months old, this Che Guevara in the making, this tatterdemalion in the preliminary throes of bulimia, had made her first statement about how she feels about the country of her birth. It won't be long before she's taunting riot squads and toting around gigantic puppet heads in vile parody of Australia's great conservative leaders. It's just a matter of time. By the time she's a teenager, she'll be standing over the Australian flag, legs akimbo, emptying her bowels all over the Southern Cross.

I hurled a dart at the nasty little miscreant. Got her right in the eye, too. She must learn that her actions have consequences, something her drugged-out parents no doubt will be loathe to impart.

Any smelly hippy with a Bic lighter and an urgent need to defecate can buy an Australian flag, unfold it outside the shop and befoul it before setting it alight.

Unless there's a total fire ban, the police are unable to do anything but sit idly by and witness the desecration. Apparently our lawmakers see nothing wrong with hippies wiping their crusted backsides on an incinerated Australian flag.

Men and women from previous generations fought and died for our flag. Well, not my parents, who fought proudly for the anti-communist movement in Germany in the 1930s and '40s, and had their own flags and symbols. But back then lots of Australian people did fight and die for the Australian flag. They must be livid to see it used in this way.

There's always been moaning from the left that the Australian flag enshrines our Anglo-Saxon heritage. Aside from replacing the Union Jack in the top left-hand corner with the motto 'Lebs Go Home', I can't see any need for a change. I'm really more Saxon than Anglo and I have never felt threatened by a symbol of the cursed British in the left-hand corner.

The left-wing moon-bats will tell you that the Union Jack appears on the flag of a handful of nations around the world, still cowering before their British colonial masters.

They want the Union Jack on the Australian flag replaced by a kangaroo or a bong or something. And as usual, they entirely miss the point.

Rather than change our flag, I say we petition the New Zealand Government to change theirs, in order to prevent any further confusion. Maybe a sheep and gumboots on a puce background would send a better message to the world. And wouldn't it look good flying above Wellington's absurd beehive parliamentary building?

The governments of the British Virgin Islands, the Falklands, Montserrat, the Cook Islands and a handful of South Pacific dungheaps laughingly referred to as sovereign nations will do as they're told: change your flag or you'll be treading water for the next couple of centuries. Our home is girt by sea, just like yours, but when it comes to acreage, we'll have a bit more up our sleeve if that global warming thing kicks in.

The rest of the world will step back in awe of the Australian flag. Not a single one of them would dare to sully it. We will have a tougher fight on our hands convincing the hippies here at home to keep the flag free of their bodily wastes. But I know a certain one-eyed neonate who now understands the dangers of defiling the Australian flag.

This article was tattooed on the gut of a 120-kilogram pig, referred to affectionately by pig farmer Nick Constantinides as A114.

The Coat of Arms

The first Australian coat of arms was issued by Edward VII by royal warrant in 1908. Edward VII was a womanising drunkard; a walking chancre who'd lay his loins on the first farm animal that wandered past. In all other respects, he was a complete bastard. He gave the thumbs up to the insipid motto on our coat of arms, which reads 'Advance Australia', as if the nation was looking to borrow a few bob from the rest of the world.

The Australian Coat of Arms: just plain wrong

Now, with the nation well on its way, and no longer in need of aging, syphilitic monarchs for inspiration, I say it's time for a change. We should arsehole the kangaroo and emu from the coat of arms. The roo and emu are dour and humourless beasts; they can't walk backwards and they'll never buy you a drink. But what critter should take their place? I think we need look no further than the beloved cane toad.

The cane toad gives a great deal of itself and expects little in return. Bufotoxin, the milky secretion oozing out of an adult cane toad, is Mother Nature's answer to LSD. Now, licking toads is a criminal offence in three states. For the uninitiated, toad licking is a dangerous activity that can send some into a psychotic spiral, rather like having *The Exorcist* on shuffle and repeat in your mind's eye for the remainder of your days. But for the rest of us, it's a bit of harmless fun. Just don't try the brown toad juice. I tried it once and, well, all I can say is I awoke in a ditch with my pants around my ankles, covered in a thick film of spiders. At least they looked like spiders.

The facts are that 102 cane toads, or *Bufo marinus* to the science geeks, came to Australia in a shoebox with some holes punched in the top way back in 1935, to wipe out, once and for all, the scourge of the cane-beetle. The toads promptly climbed out of the box and munched the cane-beetle to oblivion. They did as they were asked and they did it without complaint.

The problem is they did the job asked of them by the nation too well. And are we going to blame them for that? Some of these toads are 14,693rd generation Australians. Do we frog- or toad-march these lovable beasts off to Nauru and ask them a lot of impertinent questions as to why they feel they should be given a visa?

The cane toad is a party toad. It's settled right into the Australian way of life. It loves a drink and a root, as we all do. I'm not saying that we have to bed these critters down, tuck them in and give them a loving peck on the wart every night. There's plenty of them around, always will be, so it's okay to perform the classic cover drive on a few of them from time to time.

Of course the nay-sayers in the community now point to the fact that the cane toad has become so voracious that it is wiping out our local fauna. But let's face it: most of them are clearly not up to the pace of twenty-first century life. The toad is Darwinism in its simplest and purest form. And it's the way it has to be. And if it weren't thus we'd be up to our eye teeth in wombats the size of Volkswagens.

I've been agitating for a change to the coat of arms at the highest levels for years now and thanks to some strong support from the premier of Queensland, it finally looks like a goer. Plans are afoot to have the toad appear on the national crest, oozing bufotoxin from its leathery hide, perhaps with a walking-stick and a natty pair of sunglasses, staring maliciously into the foreground directly above the motto, 'Don't Step On Us'.

CHAPTER TWO

The Feds

If They Didn't Have Our Taxes, the Tip Would Be Full of Them

Political Parties (Beware: Voting Encourages Them)

Nowadays, the Australian party system resembles an obscure suburban footy comp with two dominant teams and a handful of easybeats who are routinely humiliated at the ballot box but keep coming back for more with a cheerfulness that can be disconcerting.

If having to vote for them weren't bad enough, Australians are required to fork out their hard-earned in electoral funding to keep political parties on a diet of schooners and swan.

The Australian Labor Party

From the Cream of the Working Class to the Dregs of the Middle Class

The Labor Party has never done a day's work in its life. It is the oldest political party in Australia, founded by a couple of shearers who, in the twilight of the nineteenth century, told their employers to go to buggery and got on the piss under the shade of a gum tree.

The tree, now 150 years old, entered the mythology of left-wing politics to become known as the Tree of Knowledge; a symbol reminding the faithful that direct political action and a few days on the drink can sort out just about anything.

Tragically, the Tree of Knowledge was poisoned in order to provide the people of Barcaldine in central Queensland with uninterrupted ocean views.

The Tree of Knowledge in Queensland: monument to the 'can do' attitude of the ALP

The ALP initially promoted such fanciful ideas as social justice and equity. After suffering repeated failure at the ballot box for the best part of eight decades, the penny finally dropped. A reformed ALP now stands on a rigid platform of economic profligacy, which essentially involves handing out cash in brown paper bags to film producers every couple of years to make films that critics declare 'unmissable' but no-one else bothers to see.

The Hawke/Keating years were a golden age for Labor. Those two were a big success, insofar as they drove us into the worst downturn since the Great Depression and still managed not to be eviscerated by an angry public.

Hawkie was a real charmer for a while. He put his hand up the nation's skirt and we loved it.

The Keating years in particular were ones of real achievement: we almost got a republic, we got a defence treaty with Indonesia that lasted four whole years, and we got the Mabo legislation (largely dismantled by the Howard Government, but still, it was a nice gesture to the blackfellas).

These days the ALP is devoid of any real policy structure. Its decision-makers now keep a steely gaze on the fax machine for policy announcements from the Liberal Party, just so they don't look like they're totally out of ideas.

Recruiting its candidates from such august bodies as the trade union movement and student politics, for years the party has been represented by every jumped-up socialist who ever ran a chook raffle at a piss-up and buggered it up. But with the demise of compulsory student unionism and the leadership of the trade union movement getting dumber by the moment, the dearth of talent within the party has forced the number crunchers to parachute ABC on-air weather presenters in to fill the yawning gap in talent.

These days the party apparatchiks look upon their own membership with a mix of disgust and deep worry. Look at the branch meetings: who wants to go out on a wet Tuesday evening to hang out with a bunch of disgruntled schoolteachers who think economic policy means writing cheques off the national budget for any interest group that comes along with a tear in its eye? These days all that's left of this once-great party are freaks, inbreds and several thousand honoured guests from the ethnic community, all with the same surname.

The Greatest Day of My Life

The America's Cup victory in 1983 was the highlight of Hawkie's prime ministership. It was one of those moments where I suddenly became a hinge upon which the whole of Australian history would turn.

When *Australia II* got over the line, I was sitting there, right beside him on the fold-up chairs. Bob was as full as a fat girl's sock, and unsure of what to say to the media.

'Give them the day off,' I whispered.

Bob grinned, then he turned around and barked, 'Any boss who sacks anyone for not turning up for work today is a bum!'

Cheers all round. Someone poured beer all over our heads. It was the greatest day of my life.

Hawkie, moments before I gave him a beer shampoo

The ALP frequently despairs of finding anyone in the membership who looks like a normal human being to run for preselection. No wonder New South Wales secretary Mark Arbib came home one night, plonked himself in front of the telly, saw the weatherman and thought, 'Shit, he'll do . . . He can wear a suit and talk at the same time. Let's bung him in North Sydney.' The light on the hill has now been replaced by an insect zapper, buzzing away in the pizza shop of naked self-interest.

The Origins of the Labor Party
And My Very Significant Role in It

AND LO there was injustice upon the land and thus mighty tectonic forces shifted and compressed the elements beneath with tremendous force into the lava of outrage which then erupted upon the face of the earth.

And God looked upon this edifice and pronounced it good and men called it THE LABOR PARTY because its creation was so utterly fucking painful and protracted.

And men and women of Australia gasped in awe at its sheer awesomeness because there really is no other word for it, and for the promise it held for the little folk, the undertrodden, the misshapen and the dwarf-like. And they had tears in their little eyes, tiny tears of hope that justice may at last run down to them like a mighty river from the likes of Wayne Swan and Morris Iemma.

And the greatest visionaries amongst the people, the wise men, the learned men, who weren't exactly labourers themselves but knew well of their plight for they had been to uni, they came forth and claimed this great edifice as their own . . .

Here it seems I must cut this short at the insistence of Random House's editors, who insist there is not 'the space' to publish my epic history of the ALP in full. And the months I spent translating Hansard into sonnet form? Well they tell me there's no room for that either. It's a sad fucking day comrade when even book publishers are captive to the sound bite and the two-second attention span. Do you suppose Alexander Pope had to put up with this? Well I'm not going to dot-point the achievements of Curtin, Chif and Gough for a bunch of Sapphic drudges. So let's just leave it there, shall we?

Here endeth the fucking lesson. And so it goes . . . and so it goes . . .

In its annual cricket match against the Canberra press corps in 1973, the ALP was dismissed for just 13 runs with the Minister for Minerals and Energy, Rex Connor, top scoring with 4 runs. Fortunately, Pakistani financier Tirath Khemlani spent the day at the scorer's table with his abacus. The Labor pollies came away with a victory by an innings and 175 runs.

Great Beards in Labor History

In the real world, people with beards are rightly regarded with some suspicion, and this is true even for men. Fortunately the ALP has always proclaimed itself a home for eccentrics with a commitment to facial hair and government control of the means of production. Here's a tasty sample of some of these great Labor beards . . .

Barry Jones

Gareth Evans

Dick 'Grizzly' Adams

Moss Cass

Don Dunstan

Labor Leaders

When Kim Beazley took over the Labor leadership after the 1996 debacle, someone said that he was the first ALP leader without a major personality disorder since the war.

Evatt was barking mad. Calwell was criminally stupid. Whitlam and Hawke had messiah complexes. Hayden was a gibbering paranoid. Keating thought you could kill cancer cells by jumping on a trampoline.

Crean was a walking ALP policy brochure, so people knew instantly he stood resolutely for nothing, and Latham was as crazy as a rat in a coffee can. His electoral platform of compulsory rugby league, home haircuts, and reading hardware catalogues to children at night delivered the train wreck the party had to have in the 2004 election.

Kevvy Rudd: continuing a fine tradition of barking mad Labor leaders

Both in chronological and physical terms, Bomber Beazley stood either side of Crean and Latham. Big Kim was and is a nice bloke without any major flaws unless you describe an addiction to Tim Tam thickshakes as a psychological illness. He confirmed the party's worst fears about his normalcy by leading the ALP to two electoral defeats by that psychopathic dwarf John Howard. Kim was well on his way to a third drubbing until Kevin Rudd took over.

Fortunately I can confirm that Kevvy's as mentally incoherent as the best of Labor's leaders. Kev suffers from what experts call a 'Sméagol-Gollum disorder'. He's in constant dialogue with himself. Watch him on the *7.30 Report*.

Kerry: Let's move on to your dinner with Brian Burke . . .

Rudd: Look, am I embarrassed by that? Yes I am. In hindsight, should I have declined the invitation? Yes I should have. Will I take a hit in the polls? Yes, I believe I will.

As you can see, the man is running an ongoing dialogue between Good Kevin (a creature he secretly calls 'Lady Blueballs') and Bad Kevin (aka 'Dirty Barbara'). Good Kev is mostly prevalent on Tuesdays, Thursdays and weekends. Bad Kev gets Mondays, Wednesdays, Fridays and public holidays.The Rudd family have learned to live with this and the country will have to as well.

The Liberal Party

Pit Bulls of Democracy

The party of Menzies was first created to 'Appease the Japanese', which Old Ming thought was a tremendous slogan and would be a real winner with the electorate.

In order to make Howard more palatable to voters, his constant companion in the 1996 election was a giant cartoon chicken

In time, Menzies would become a Cold War warrior, happy to consign Australia's youth to wars around the globe. But in the days when the Liberal Party was a mere foetus in the womb of the unmarried teenaged mother of Australian politics, Menzies believed that Australia's best hope of overcoming Japanese expansionism in the 1930s and 1940s was for the population to gallantly lie down, while he rummaged around in the shed, boxing up and dispatching Australia's only defensive weapons to the Mother Country for the British to eat.

Menzies went on to serve Australia as prime minister for a record seventy-eight years. He held sway over the party room with a mixture of rat cunning and blunt-force trauma. Such was his hold over the party that he continued on as prime minister for seven years after his death. No-one in the Liberal Party had the temerity to poke him with a stick and check for a pulse.

One of my first jobs, fresh out of tech school as a strapping young lad with an interest in the political caper, was to administer formaldehyde enemas to Old Ming on a daily basis and carry his lifeless cadaver around in a sedan chair throughout the 1963 election campaign. The voters didn't seem to notice or mind and returned the old bugger to the top job with an increased majority.

Menzies finally retired in 1965 after one of his eyeballs fell out in a joint parliamentary sitting. Country Party leader Jack McEwen and I did the right thing and buried the smelly old bugger, wheeling his putrescent corpse out in a wheelbarrow to a hole in the ground out the back of Old Parliament House in a brief yet solemn ceremony.

Menzies created the Liberal Party as a party with family values firmly at heart. With his departure from the scene the Liberals realised the only families they gave a bugger about were their own.

Australian families were a lot of work: they were always moaning about their living standards and having their young blokes sent off to the nearest war. There was nothing else for the Liberals to do but join the warm embrace of the business community.

The Kirribilli Disagreement

I remember being called to Kirribilli House in 2006 and walking through the broken crockery, overturned furniture and shattered vases. I knew then it was over. I did my best to keep John Howard and Peter Costello together but I'd failed. It just wasn't meant to be, I suppose.

It had taken every ounce of my strength. A few months earlier the Liberal Party had asked me to step in and act as relationship counsellor for John Howard and Peter Costello. To outsiders, it just seemed that there were the usual tensions in the relationship, and that this was par for the course for all couples. That's what I thought, too. Then I sat down with them and began to get a thorough understanding of the full extent of the problem. There were enormous unresolved issues in the relationship. All this has left me very disconsolate. I found myself sitting in among the detritus of just another broken relationship, sculling Phisohex, trying to remove the foul stench of failure.

Under my firm guidance and unusual methods, I thought we were getting there; making some real progress. But on that Monday night there'd been a flare-up when Costello came home and found an emerald-studded earring on Howard's bedside table. Brendan Nelson hadn't worn an earring for two years but Costello put two and two together and came up with five. There was a hell of a blue, the police were called and by the time I got there, the PM and the treasurer were at each other's throats. It was a very ugly scene.

One of the methods I employ when couples are in crisis is the honesty session. So in the midst of all this twisted domestic wreckage, ugliness and hyper-aggression, I sat them down on the only unbroken chairs in the house and asked them both to speak honestly with each other, no taboo subjects, all cards on the table.

Well, after five minutes of long, stony silence, I realised that honesty does not come easily to this couple – gifted orators and debaters as they are. It's just not their strong suit.

With some judicious prompting from me with a cattle prod and a bucket of water, we got underway, but sadly, there was no getting away from the bitter recriminations. And when Howard got to his feet and told Costello, 'You're the worst treasurer this country has seen and that includes Billy McMahon,' I had to step in and tell them, 'Whoa, come now, let's not say anything we can't take back, here.'

Before you knew it Costello was gone in a huff. He took his CD collection and his black T-shirts, packed them up in an overnight bag and took off. He's living in a fleabag motel in Redfern now, just until he can find some permanent digs. Now, there's an AVO in place and there's really no going back from there.

Meanwhile Howard's been bugging me, telling me he thinks Costello stole his Elgar CD. He wants it back. JWH loves a bit of *Pomp and Circumstance* – he can't go a day without marching up and down the hallway to a bit of the old Elgar in that silly bloody tracksuit of his.

But the real problem is Costello is a classic passive aggressive type. For the past ten years he'd just been sitting about sullenly expecting a commitment from Howard. But Howard's not that sort of bloke. He's commitment averse. The commitment averse are always tricky to deal with for relationship counsellors like myself.

And Howard may look like he's everyone's favourite grandfather but the truth is he's got a mouth on him like Naomi Robson. When it comes to conflict resolution that sort of approach just isn't helpful.

I'm a firm believer that all successful relationships are based on a solid foundation of lies and deceit. Thus, at first at least, Howard and Costello's relationship looked like a match made in heaven.

But Costello came over all high and mighty, saying that Howard offered him a leg up twelve years ago and that Howard should be true to his word.

The truth was that Howard had been offering the top job to all and sundry for the last ten years. He told me it was mine for the taking too, if I could help him sort out his differences with Costello. When I told him I wasn't a member of parliament, he told me not to worry, that by the time he was finished as PM, it wouldn't matter.

Your Problems Solved

Problem: The Liberal leadership. No-one has the intellect, the drive, the charisma and dress sense to lead this once great party. The current crop just don't cut the mustard, I'm afraid!

Solution: Draft David Flint! Mr Flint has better diction than (sadly) just about anyone else in Australia. He's a natty dresser and he looks quite scrumptious in his tailored suits. (Are you *with me* on this one, girls?)

Method: Find him a safe seat! Simply enlist 5000 Laotian migrants to join the local branch and *instruct* them to support Mr Flint. *You must be patient.* You must be prepared to tolerate their language and their ghastly children!

Result: Mr David Flint, our next Liberal Leader! The man of the hour! After preselection for Mr Flint is accomplished, you only need to institute a simple membership requirement (say, a lamington baking test) to drive the new members out again, spit spot! It's easy!

David Flint: drool away girls

Making up the Numbers

The Greens: *Pinkos and nimbies and junkies on strings – these are a few of my least favourite things*

I've tried hard to get along with the Greens but when I saw Bob Brown in a pair of hemp chaps climbing out of a steam-driven Kombi Van, I knew in my heart I could not deal with these people. You can't do business with hippies. The best you can hope for is to rip off their stash of illicit drugs and moonshine and flog it to a few blokes you've just met at the pub.

Bob Brown: a powerful advocate for a return to the grand old days of the steam age

The Australian Democrats: *Say goodnight to all the nice people*

The party that was formed to keep the bastards honest is soon to be pronounced illegitimate by the Australian Electoral Commission. In fact, deregistration of the party is already underway in earnest.

The Democratic Labor Party: *Splitters*

Howard's vision of transporting Australia back to the 1950s was never more gruesomely realised than when the DLP bounced back after almost half a century in oblivion with the election of two members to the Victorian Upper House. It won't last, though. I've seen the DLP mailing list and it's only got three names on it. And one of those is Bob Santamaria. No, these blokes can't survive in the vibrant political landscape of twenty-first century Australia. Not unless North Korea succeeds in exporting its peculiar form of communism to the world. And the Pope becomes pro-choice.

Steve Fielding and his wife Susan: every Sunday morning around at your place

Family First: *God-botherers now bothering voters*

A party that's all about sending people to Canberra, in the certain knowledge they'll never see their families again. These people are major nuisances: they'll come doorknocking at 7 am on a Sunday before you've had time to shoo the hookers out of the house. Having said that, I have a fair bit of respect for these relentless, homophobic God-botherers. They somehow managed to get Steve Fielding elected to the senate in 2004, even though he only received a handful of votes from disenchanted carnie folk. Any party that can stitch up that kind of preference deal deserves a round of applause.

One Nation: *Transcending the merely factual*

Pauline Hanson gave her party this name before someone advised her that Australia had already federated. By then it was too late. It didn't matter. Pauline's great gift to politics is that she transcends the merely factual and addresses her people from a much higher plane, speaking in riddles like a Zen Buddhist monk. Recently she lashed out at Muslims, but declared that Christian Muslims were okay. Her devoted acolytes are still trying to figure that one out.

Pauline Hanson confounded critics and fans alike with an interfaith message of love for all the people of the world

The Prime Minister

On a Throne of Pain, atop a Mountain of Skulls

Ben Chifley: his thunderous bowel explosions kept many travelling salesmen awake at night

We should raffle the political leadership of this country. First prize a tray of chops from Brown's Quality Slaughterhouse and Butchery and second prize the keys to the Lodge. You've got to be in it to win it and tickets would be available to all interested punters at local pubs and RSLs throughout the nation. Fifty cents a ticket or fifteen for five bucks.

Frankly, you'd stand a better chance of becoming prime minister if the job was raffled off. To become a prime minister in the present shambles you have to be: 1) a politician; 2) a member of federal parliament; 3) a member of the government; 4) a member of Cabinet; and 5) hold a current forklift licence.

And even if you've got all your ducks in a row, you've still got to hack and slash away at your colleagues for years and years before you are even considered an outside chance for the top job. This is especially true when you find yourself a lowly minister in the outer cabinet – the Minister Responsible for Raking the Sand in the Parliamentary Ashtrays or something even more horrible: the Minister for Aged Care.

The good news is once you've cleaved a path through the party room and clambered your way over the corpses, there's no-one to stop you from parking your arse in the big chair. But once you're there, you've got to keep a constant eye out for the next crop of ugly, ambitious swine, keen to turf you out and give you a damned good kicking on the way.

When Ben Chifley was prime minister, he knocked back bed and breakfast at the Lodge, preferring to bunk in at a local private hotel. His room didn't have a bath or a brasco. So it was not unusual for travelling salesmen to be having a shave and a wash in the morning while Chif backed one out in the middle cubicle.

Nowadays, it's chauffeur-driven limos, your very own RAAF burner and all the swan you can eat.

There are plenty of perks but the downside is the money's not great. You're on call twenty-four hours a day and there are no shift allowances or RDOs. Pro rata, Australian prime ministers earn only slightly more than the young sheila knocking out smoothies at the local Boost juice.

I don't recommend it to young kiddies looking for a career but if you're absolutely determined to have a crack at becoming prime minister, be prepared for a long trip. Best take a good book.

The Cabinet

The Dark Enclosed Box from which the Nation is Governed

6 months in	Everything's sweetness and light. The prime minister and treasurer form a great partnership. Ministers are 'pleasantly surprised' at how good the PM is as chair of Cabinet. The PM brings in some lamingtons to share, just to show, you know, that he's not up himself and that. There's a little strain because the treasurer has somehow 'discovered' a 986 bazillion dollar black hole in the budget left by the previous government and everyone's going to have to come up with some cuts. But ministers are just happy that they don't have to catch taxis any more.
12 months in	One year in and it's clear that a couple of Cabinet members have no media skills and that they simply have to go. The PM gives broad hints by bringing out his guitar and singing Cat Stevens songs whenever these ministers are speaking. The PM looks to the outer ministry and comes to the grim realisation that some of his junior ministers are full of hate and have all the morals of a virus. These people are quickly promoted into Cabinet to replace the duds with no media skills.
24 months in	Cabinet meets less and less often. Ministers show up sporting physical scars as their marriages deteriorate. The PM is increasingly contemptuous of Cabinet government, showing a tendency to roll his eyes and say, 'like, whatever . . .' to his colleagues. The great partnership between the PM and his treasurer is definitely over. The treasurer realises the vague assurances given to him by the PM that he will stand aside are worthless. The PM wants the treasurer to understand that the national emergency created by last year's Great Stationery Crisis obliges him to stay on in the national interest. The treasurer starts to feel uncomfortable walking into the Cabinet room as everyone is giggling and staring at him.
30 months in	Cabinet government is effectively over by now. Everything is run from the PM's office. Ministers are informed of crucial decisions that affect their department by SMS or by watching the news crawl on *Sunrise* with Mel and Kochie.

Parliament

It's All About Putting Bums On Seats

About the only good thing about being a parliamentarian is no-one cares if you don't turn up.

Aside from that, being elected to federal parliament is the worst thing that can ever happen to you, short of death.

Back when you were elected, you felt like you were the cock of the walk. It must be reassuring to learn that approximately 50 per cent of your neighbours don't despise you.

Commonwealth Parliament: and you thought being a lawyer was bad

But once you get to Canberra that euphoria will quickly disappear, replaced by a terrible sense that you don't belong.

While preparing your maiden speech – an embarrassing ramble about what wonderful people your parents are and how you've never let them feel guilty for keeping you restrained in an upturned clothes hamper for the first four years of your life – it suddenly occurs to you that your children did not even shift their gaze from the television to say goodbye when the taxi turned up to take you to the airport last night.

And just when you thought things couldn't get any worse, the party whip pays you a visit lugging a pair of boltcutters. You are firmly reminded of your obligations to the party and what will happen to you should you forget, even for a moment.

The party whip bids you farewell after snipping you for two grand for the footy tipping. While counting the money, he explains you have no prospect of winning because it's the treasurer's turn to pocket the prize. He stops at the door on the way out to tell you to 'pull your head in'.

You could go and work some of the pain out at the parliamentary gym but the thought of touching anything that Tony Abbott or Lindsay Tanner has sweated on fills you with revulsion. You could go to the dining room and get a bite to eat but you're pretty sure the catering staff are spitting in your food.

And then suddenly you bow your head and weep helplessly, hopelessly, at the utter awfulness of it all.

Welcome to the Big House. The first three years are always the hardest.

Parliament House, Canberra: the most horrible place on earth

AUSTRALIAN DEMOCRACY
An Outsider's View

George W. Bush, President of the United States of America

Dateline October 23, 2003, 2:30am AEST
President George W. Bush arrives in Canberra to address federal parliament. The Usher of the Black Rod approaches the chamber door and taps on it three times with his staff before impatient US marines kick it open, enter the chamber and arrest everyone of Middle Eastern appearance. Joe Hockey, Daryl Melham, Santo Santoro and Sophie Panopoulos are ordered at gunpoint to strip to their underpants and form a human pyramid in front of the Speaker's Chair.

The president jogs into the chamber wearing sneakers, shorts and iPod to 'Eye of the Tiger'. He clambers to the top of the human pyramid and speaks from his heart to the Australian people.

George Bush: a Great Australian

President BUSH *(R-Texas)*
My fellow Americans.

Nervous giggles from the government benches.

President BUSH
Lookin' out here at you folks with your smilin' faces, I got two words to say to you: woo-hoo!

Mr DOWNER *(Mayo, Minister for Foreign Affairs)*
Woo-hoo!

President BUSH
Can't hear ya . . .

Several members enthusiastically cheer, 'Woo-hoo'.

President BUSH
Let me state once again to you Prime Minister Howard, my sincere thanks for your hospitality.

Mr HOWARD (Bennelong, Prime Minister) scratches himself and gurgles with pleasure.

President BUSH
You know I call him the Man of Steel. That's because he makes a kinda 'clanky-clanky' sound when he walks.

It's a pleasure to be here with you and to inhale the rich smell of democracy. And I gotta tell you, Australia's come a long way for a country that was, let's be frank, the birthplace of Hitler and an enthusiastic participant in the Third Reich and all. But you're democratic now and I say let bygones be bygones.

Mr LATHAM *(Werriwa, Shadow Treasurer)*
You deadshit. I spit on the graves of your war dead.

Eight marines pounce and place Mr Latham in a Hannibal Lecter–style cage. Order is restored.

President BUSH
You got yourselves a different system here to the one we got back home. And I gotta say, I like it. Back home, we call our parliament the 'Congress'.

President Bush presses button and PowerPoint slide appears above Speaker's chair with the words 'THE CONGRESS'.

President BUSH
And this 'Congress' makes a big deal about bein' independent of the executive. That makes my job awful hard. Every year the 'president' (that's me) prepares a budget that looks like a gourmet meal. Then I feed it to the 'Congress', and when it comes out the other end six months later, well, it don't look or smell very nice.

Senators Bob Brown and Kerry Nettle, in protest against the Reagan Administration's funding of contra activity in Nicaragua, douse themselves with fuel from the parliamentary petrol can and self-immolate.

President BUSH
Anyhoo. Here, I'm told it's different. Your prime minister, he gets to do what he likes, short of stickin' kids from Third World countries in open-ended detention, before anyone starts to cough nervously in the party room.

Strong applause from government benches. Opposition reluctantly joins the applause after receiving some sharpish looks from Foreign Minister Downer.

President BUSH
Woo-hoo! So although both our great nations have different systems, both systems were designed by men of genius, men of great vision.

President Bush displays PowerPoint slide of Washington, Jefferson and Geraldo Rivera.

CHAPTER THREE

The States

All Australians are Equal, Some Australians are More Equal than Others

New South Wales

Motto	Unmarked notes, if you don't mind
Faunal Emblem	Crapweed
Floral Emblem	Race 4 No. 5

Fair dinkum, it makes my heart pump purple piss when I think about how New South Wales is run these days.

Back when Liberal premier Sir Robert Askin was running the show, you could spend the morning dotting the i's and crossing the t's on a deal while having a sauna and a rubdown with vicious criminals, some very polite Asian girls, one or two ideologically flexible politicians and the chief commissioner of police. When we got the business stuff out of the way, there was always plenty of time for a long lunch and a day at the races before we went back to Asko's favourite brothel for a long lie-down.

I could tell you all about how the state government works now but the truth is they're not in charge. New South Wales is run by Lebanese crime gangs. And credit where it's due, the Beirut Boys have shown a bit of flair for affairs of state. But it's something of a closed shop and although I always keep an eye on the want ads, they never seem to be hiring.

The state that gave us Asko, two hundred years of systemic police corruption and the Big Merino is now a shadow of itself, run by clowns who wouldn't know how to place a boxed trifecta, let alone rig a race so the nags would trot along comfortably in set formation to the finishing post.

The only bloke who's made any sense in politics since Asko died of Spanish Dancer was Nifty Nev Wran. Wran was a bloke who understood politics and what people wanted from it. Confirming the existence of the divide between church and state, Nev once remarked, 'If the greedy bastards wanted spirituality, they'd go for the Hare fucking Krishnas.' He was utterly right, of course and the people of New South Wales understood it immediately.

Sydney is so riven by provincialism that people who live in the eastern suburbs would prefer to catch a burner to Liechtenstein than cross the bridge and actually talk to someone from the North Shore.

Nifty knew that better than anyone: he made his own long journey from his poor-as-shit childhood in Balmain to the 'leafy' eastern suburbs. But he never forgot where he came from. And so, as premier, Nifty swore to end poverty in Balmain. And he did: by giving poor families a key to a housing commission flat and a bus ticket to Mt Druitt. This had the happy side effect of creating Lebensraum in Balmain for his colleagues in advertising and the legal profession.

Asko doing the form on Saturday morning: he was a genius on the punt

Great Insiders: Sir Robert Askin
Premier of New South Wales 1965–1975

The following was delivered as a eulogy for the former New South Wales premier by Jack the Insider

The petty and mean-spirited administrators of the day denied Sir Robert, a premier of New South Wales for a near-record eleven years, his God-given right to a state funeral. Nevertheless as his funeral cortege meandered slowly through the streets of Sydney on that bleak day, people flocked in their thousands to witness the great man's passing into the history books, proving once and for all that if you give the public what they want, they'll come out and make a day of it.

Sir Robert William Askin has mysteriously been overlooked in the rush to deify others who held public office with less aplomb and devotion to duty. I feel it is down to me to restore this great man's reputation and his legacy of integrity and accountability.

Sir Robert was a man of courage: a man who stood fast, with his left hand held high, as if to say, 'The Liberal Party is not for sale.'

However he did advise that it was available for hire, on surprisingly modest terms. By the simple act of leaving a brown paper bag in the third stall in the toilets on the mezzanine at Central Station, one could have a real piece of participatory democracy in this state. Sir Robert's driver would collect the largesse, stopping only to run over a couple of nay-saying hippy types, who clearly did not understand what the great man was all about.

Bob Askin was a visionary. He could tell you the winner and the two placegetters of a horse race before it even started, after receiving a phone call on his private line from Perce Galea.

Tough on crime, tougher on the causes of crime, Bob Askin assembled a crack team to wipe out the menace of criminals who refused to contribute to police superannuation funds.

And when the merry-go-round of party politics finally stopped to let Sir Robert Askin off, he had the considerable foresight to die before the plod arrived to knock down his door, handcuff the old bugger and then make way for the Australian Taxation Office to enter and gnaw on his wife's near-dead carcass.

It's said that the great man's ghost haunts the corridors of the New South Wales Parliament; a place where he once did battle with his many political foes, where he copped a quid and the odd tip on the races with a gentle dignity, and with a stroke of a legislative pen created such notable infrastructure features as the Cahill Expressway and introduced the cool, classic lines of Soviet architecture to Kings Cross.

Yet when I cast an eye across this once fine state, I see no edifice, no statue, no monument, to his manifest achievements. It is for this reason that I hereby dedicate the third stall in the toilets on the mezzanine at Central Station in his honour. It shall from this day forth be known as The Asko Memorial Brasco so that when the people of New South Wales feel so inclined they may sit, reflect and, when so moved, offer up their movements by way of thanks to one of the state's great premiers.

New South Wales during Askin's reign: it was a golden age

Askin had managed to stick his drinking straw in the giant public milkshake for years and no-one said a thing. Nick Greiner lost the premiership because his own commission found he'd been 'technically corrupt'! This was a sign of creeping wowserism in this once great state.

I'm technically drunk right now but that doesn't mean I'm going to shirk my responsibilities and go and get a cushy job in the tobacco industry.

In Nifty's time the people of New South Wales would happily enjoy a beer and a day at the races. They'd still be at the races too, if Bob Carr hadn't come along and started sucking up to the Hillsong kiddies. Ironically, Carr had read a few books on Christianity while enjoying a day at the races and thought there might be a few votes in it for him.

He started turning up at their shows, strumming guitars and praising the Lord. He even spoke in tongues once but that was at a parliamentary inquiry into the toll roads around Sydney. No-one could understand a word he was saying and he walked out the door grinning his arse off.

Carr was a secret member of the cult of the shrunken head (see Victoria). That's why he got the nod to host the most successful Olympic Games in history. Over ten glorious days, Sydneysiders flocked in their thousands to watch steroid-enriched Senegalese runners panting around a track. The whole thing was book-ended with some gay blokes on horseback and Kylie on a giant thong. It was great.

Every nation fell in love with Sydney and they're now sending us their gregarious young folk to serve us beers and keep the box jellyfish well fed.

JOBS FOR THE BOYS

At the Sydney 2000 Olympics, the Armenian wrestling team ran into trouble with immigration officials when they headed out for a steam and sauna to ease their aching muscles. They entered a known homosexual haunt in Oxford Street and remained there for the next four years. After his arrest and detention, super heavyweight Greco-Roman wrestler Dimitri Slagaboff obtained a resident visa and is now employed as a towel boy at the club.

Queensland

Motto	Open for business
Faunal Emblem	Something nice, y'know. Something imported.
Floral Emblem	Fine Cotton

The people of Queensland are as docile as buggery. I like to think of them as being like box jellyfish, inert and at peace for the most part until someone pokes them with a stick and they turn ugly and violent and will have your kids' eyes out in a heartbeat.

They're funny buggers, Queenslanders. They're happy to sell the state off to the Japanese and Chinese but become incandescent with rage when ever they lose a sporting tournament to New South Wales.

They've always had an inferiority complex. They look at the people from the southern states and drop their heads to the floor, feeling like they're playing for the reserves, culturally speaking.

But Queenslanders are way off the mark. The state has got culture coming out of its arse. The Gold Coast is my second home and I'm here to tell you that it's a cultural Mecca. Only on the Gold Coast you don't have so many Arab kiddies throwing rocks and generally running around making nuisances of themselves.

Right slap-bang in the middle of the Gold Coast is the Raptis Plaza, with the second largest Woolworths in the Southern Hemisphere. And just out the front, there's Michelangelo's *David*. Well, not THE *David* by Michelangelo but a better one: newer, bigger, whiter, and one where the local artist has very thoughtfully knocked up a decent todger on the lad rather than the sad thing Michelangelo fashioned with a hammer and chisel all those years ago.

Michelangelo's *David*: deeply unsatisfying, but the one at Surfers Paradise has come up trumps

Queensland is the home of the eccentric politician. For years I've had to deal with a bunch of blokes in silly hats and sheilas who'd be better suited to knocking out real estate in Toowoomba than running the state but I've always found them agreeable and easy to get along with. Unlike some I could mention, Queensland politicians aren't people who feel restricted by moral encumbrances, preferring to get on and do a bit of business.

You could trace it all back to Vince Gair's premiership of Queensland back in the 1950s. Very sensibly, in my view, Vince Gair decided the Labor Party had outlived its usefulness. Vince tore up his ALP membership, got some hookers in and a crate of long necks and came up with a party all of his own. He was like that, old Vince.

Hinze Dam has a capacity of over 140 million litres, which is exactly how much piss Russ and I knocked back while he was Minister for Everything

It buggered the Labor Party's chance of getting elected anywhere for the next fifteen years and Vince got so drunk that he had to accept a diplomatic post as Ambassador to Ireland and the Holy See, just to dry out for a while.

In 1968, Joh Bjelke-Petersen got elected as premier and rigged up a gerrymander so that his government would continue to be returned for the best part of three decades. Joh did this by ensuring that a mate of his called Des, who lived in Kingaroy, cast the only vote that counted in Queensland.

People moan about Joh but the truth is his government did a great deal to wipe the scourge of prostitution off the face of the map. Or at least keep it confined to a lively Tuesday night at Russ Hinze's house once a week.

And they invested millions in infrastructure. It was my idea to commence construction on the Hinze Dam and build it as a 1:1 scale model of the big fella himself.

Nowadays, Hinze Dam is as dry as a chip and about one tenth of the size it used to be. Russ has been dead for a while, so I suppose in an odd sort of way there's still a striking resemblance.

A MARVEL OF AUSTRALIAN INFRASTRUCTURE

The Dingo Fence stretches 5320 kilometres from Jimbour on the Darling Downs near Dalby through thousands of miles of arid country to the Eyre Peninsula on the Great Australian Bight. It is the only dingo fence in the world visible from the moon.

The legacy of the Joh government can still be seen today. There are 1500 people a week venturing across the Tweed for a bit of sun and a lie-down on a banana lounge who refuse to do the right thing and leave. It wouldn't be happening if Russ Hinze was still Minister for Everything. If Russ was still running the show, he'd build a wall to keep those bloody southerners out and name it after himself, of course.

THE JOH THAT I KNEW

Sir Johannes Bjelke-Petersen, Premier of Queensland 1968–1987

Sir Joh was, after Jesus Christ and Phar Lap, the greatest man who ever lived.

In the seventies and eighties most Australians could only envy Queenslanders and their Canny Leader, who saw the establishment in this country for what it is: a vast conspiracy of Giant Yellow Lizards to defraud us of our natural wealth. Sir Joh never actually said that in public, but he believed it.

Let me tell you how I came to know the great man.

Back in 1988, when Sir Joh was finally undone by his enemies, he had to be physically evicted from the Premier's Office. He was bloodied but unbowed. He tried his hand as an entrepreneur, and he cheerfully announced that his new company would sell you anything from a 'jumbo jet to a combine harvester'.

I shot off a letter to Sir Joh and I told him I thought he was brought down by a Giant Yellow Lizard conspiracy. He wrote straight back and said that I was spot on, and by the way would I care to purchase a jumbo jet from him?

After I sent him a couple of substantial down payments, Joh rang to say that the Lizards had now bankrupted him and I wouldn't be getting my jet after all. I told him not to worry; it was just like the Lizards to do something like that and my five kids and two ex-wives would now have to work for a living.

Today you can see proof of Joh's greatness in the Brisbane skyline. Them skyscrapers would not be there today if Joh hadn't shown up on site at 6 am every day with a few coppers, ready to put a bullet into any worker who looked like becoming a shop steward.

In his heyday, lesser, more timid figures would beg Joh to 'reach out across the divide'. Joh's response was just superb. He said: 'You can't walk along a barbed-wire fence with a foot in each paddock.' He was right as always; at first thought it seems a harmless, playful exercise, but I know for a fact it's deeply painful and may even cause long-term damage to your lolly bag.

Sir Joh: the man kept a constant look out for Lizard activity

South Australia

Motto	Never mind the price, feel the quality
Faunal Emblem	Gigantic Maralinga butterbeans, as big as your head
Floral Emblem	Twee platypi fashioned in earthenware on a raffia base. Ten dollars, cash, and that's my last word

South Australia has been run by a shadowy group known as 'The Downer Family' for the best part of 150 years. It's impossible for anyone else to get a look in.

Not that South Australia can afford to do without a man like me greasing the wheels of industry. South Australia is a basket case. There's very little work going on there to speak of, since they tidied up the green fluorescent rocks around Maralinga and popped them in the wastepaper basket.

SA Premier Mike Rann and NT Chief Minister Clare Martin pick up a bit of work on the railways

It's got so bad that the current premier, Mike Rann, now works part time and pops in to the office just on Wednesdays to check his emails. He's got a bit of job share going with a pregnant sheila who works at the local Red Rooster, so he's able to make ends meet.

Rather than get stuck into a bit of manufacturing, like they used to in the old days, South Australians have tried to kick-start the state economy by creating a bunch of festivals, so they can get drunk for days on end.

I've been to a few of these festivals and always profoundly enjoyed my time there. Sadly though, whenever the South Australians come up with a really good idea for a piss-up, the Victorians pinch the concept and whack it in over the Melbourne Cup weekend to stop the tourists from sobering up and seeing for themselves what an awful place they're staying in.

South Australia prides itself on being a state of liberalism and progressive politics. It was the first place in Australia to give women the vote. And the womenfolk, chuffed with their new tool of electoral power, rewarded the very nice gesture by voting for a series of conservative governments – the very same conservative governments that thought women's suffrage would lead to hell in a hand basket – for the next eighty years.

Adelaide was settled in the post World War II period by immigrants too ugly and violent for Glasgow. The outer suburbs in the city's north became home to these malcontents. Bereft of services like public transport and public health, the émigrés found their niche in the hastily knocked up ghettos, began strumming guitars and got so bloody good at it they would rule the radio waves in Australia for the next fifty years.

Too deep: a large hole like this one in Snowtown will generally attract the attention of the police

The shallow grave was invented in South Australia and is still the preferred method of corpse disposal throughout the state.

Further up the road is the Barossa Valley, a place I have a deep and abiding affection for. I like to spend a few weeks there every year, strapped to a 500-litre oak cask and a funnel.

But beware, if you drive any further north, you'll come to Maralinga and if you manage to get that far, my strong advice to you is keep the windows wound up.

Tasmania

Motto	Remember us?
Faunal Emblem	The Huon Pine (a photograph of which can be seen in Tasmanian Museum of Natural History)
Floral Emblem	~~Thylacine~~, ~~Tasmanian Devil~~, David Boon

Tasmanians are living proof that ignoring people in the hope they will go away doesn't always work.

Tasmania is the home of green politics in Australia and stands as a shining example of how awful life could be if we gave the Greens any more than 10 per cent of the vote. Fortunately, the leader of the Greens, Dr Bob Brown, is proof positive that being gay does not necessarily make you interesting.

The Tasmanian economy relies solely on an aging hippy who makes muesli from his own faeces and flogs it in hemp sacks out of the boot of his car down at the Salamanca markets every Saturday morning.

After he experienced a particularly nasty spate of constipation in the winter of 2003, supply of the muesli became erratic and unreliable. The crisis led to the intervention of the World Bank, who caught the ferry across from Victoria, had a look around and quickly left, heading to Burundi, figuring at least they could do some good in central Africa.

Hippies have little to do in Tasmania but indoctrinate youngsters and thus their vile hemp-wearing ways are perpetuated

The Tasmanians were the first state to knock up a legal casino and for years Wrest Point in Hobart was the jewel of the island. I used to get down there most weekends and throw a bit of money around on the Crown and Anchor. Funny, I didn't think then that it was a garish monument to all that was ugly about the 1970s.

Left to rot without refurbishment since then, the casino now stands as a ghastly cultural museum – a reminder of the wanton excesses of soft furnishings back then. Just last year I took a stroll on the electric green carpet and noticed with horror the burnt-orange flock wallpaper and tartan beanbags. 'What the hell were these people thinking?'

I went upstairs to the revolving rooftop restaurant and necked a few schooners. I noticed that the motor which makes the thing spin around in a way that was a marvel of modern science in 1979 is now so clunky and turns so slowly you can observe that homes in Sandy Bay could do with a lick of paint since you saw them on the last lap around.

The current premier, Paul Lennon, may be the most hideous dandy seen in this country since Alan Jones first tried on a pink chemise to wear with his canary yellow cashmere cardigan. I've been telling Lennon for years to get himself a black Delmonti suit and thin tie but he just won't listen.

Paul Lennon's strong view is that Tasmania's real future lies with the gambling and wagering industry. And if he gets it right, I know there'll be some corollory benefits for Tasmania's tourist industry. I know for a fact that a number of members of the Italian-American community and one or two Romanian guys are willing to jump on a burner and head down to Tasmania and help out where they can. There's nothing these guys don't know about making book and how to clear up any unwanted bad debts accrued along the way.

With an eye constantly fixed on the mainland, Tasmania flirted with the idea of political corruption, turning towards conservative automaton, Robin Gray, who very kindly agreed to pass the island over to the hydro-electrical industry on the off-chance that the Hydro Electric Commission would kick-start the economy with regular deliveries of folding stuff in brown paper bags.

Gray's romance with the dark end of business ended when the HEC agreed to cut him a cheque for seven dollars for the entire state, provided everyone agreed to leave at once and colonise Heard Island. Gray very sensibly knocked the offer back. Sadly, Tasmania has failed to progress since and now relies heavily on icebreakers returning from Antarctica for a few tourist dollars.

TASMANIA, MAP OF

For years the map of Tassie has been used as an ugly metaphor for the female pudenda by shit comics at smoke nights. The truth is that Tasmania has more in common topographically with a bulldog eating custard. If you hold the map on its side, that is. And when you think about it, the female genitalia looks a lot more like the Sea of Japan.

Victoria

Motto	Who do you barrack for then, eh? Eh?
Faunal Emblem	Bread
Floral Emblem	Circuses

If you listen very carefully in Victoria, you can still hear the sounds of banks collapsing. To this day, the credit card is almost permanently maxed out as Victorians seem peculiarly attracted to spending billions of dollars on world-class sporting, entertainment and artistic facilities that no-one ever uses.

Instead people in Victoria spend most of their time dressed entirely in black, sneering at the rest of Australia and challenging Sydney to a fight, which Sydney people ignore, having never heard of the place.

Proudly, Victorians hold up their police force as the most corrupt in the world, but the truth is, the plod in Zimbabwe probably has its nose in front. It's just another instance of Victorian hyperbole not quite matching up to reality.

I was just a kid fresh out of tech school when I applied for a job working for the then Victorian premier, Sir Henry Bolte. I was good at knots, so he gave me a gig. Back then, the irascible old bastard had implemented a series of bizarre policies which permitted him to hang people in his own garage. Parliament sat infrequently in those days, allowing Bolte to get on with the serious business of lynching ne'er-do-wells.

I had to strap these poor buggers up to his B&D Roll-A-Door so Sir Henry could dispatch them with a simple press of the remote-control door opener. It was hard work and it nearly did my back in. But Bolte never offered me any workers' compensation and I'll never forgive him for it.

In a further wanton assault on democracy, Bolte also introduced the *Shrunken Head Act 1964*, restricting the office of premier to anyone who had a head smaller than a tennis ball. Bolte remained premier for another ten years, surviving a series of party-room spills by measuring the skulls of contenders with a string on a stick.

The tiny head of state: Sir Henry Bolte

Another shrunken head premier, John Cain, was elected to power and promptly set about getting the state's finances in order by arranging a loan from a mate of mine named Vinnie, who warned Cain about what would happen if he couldn't come up with the vig. When Cain missed his monthly payment in May 1989, Vinnie marched into the State Parliament, gave the premier a damned good thrashing and set about absorbing the State Bank of Victoria into his thriving cigarette machine racket.

The Shrunken Head Act was finally repealed when Jeff Kennett emerged on the political scene with his gigantic melon. Kennett was swept to power on an enormous head platform.

Kennett and his vast cranium reformed Victoria; turning it into a vibrant tourist spot by offering visitors free flights and accommodation, as long as they spent a day at the car races with him. Kennett's period as premier was one of Victoria's most tumultuous but happily all that argy-bargy didn't distract Kennett from the real business at hand: building on his already substantial portfolio.

I remember being at a press conference where Kennett headbutted a cameraman, kicked a print journalist in the groin and told Victorians they could all get fucked. I knew then he'd gone too far. It was only a matter of time before he would be swept from power and replaced by Steve Bracks, a man with a vision for a softer, gentler Victoria and an even larger head than Kennett's, if that were possible.

Today Victoria is a lively, prosperous state with a multi-billion-dollar economy entirely powered by Victorians being forced at gunpoint onto the pokies, where they sit feverishly flushing their life savings down the brasco.

Boofhead Bracks packed it in 2007, flicking the top job onto John Brumby. Brumby has a much smaller head than his predecessor but he's a former treasurer, so he will more than make up for his cranial shortcomings with a ruthless indirect taxation regime.

THE PEOPLE OF ORBOST

Orbost in Victoria's south-west has become the most sought-after location of the world's anthropologists. Last year over 12,000 anthropologists converged on the Gippsland town of 2000, poking about with their pipe-stems and generally making nuisances of themselves.

The behavioural science atavists can be seen jostling for the best spots along the main street, while the people of Orbost get on with their day-to-day business: getting drunk and angry on Friday nights, copulating awkwardly and watching the local footy team get the shit kicked out of it on Saturday arvos.

But while the economic contribution the geeks have made is appreciated, the fact is that living under the microscope has made the town folk increasingly uncomfortable.

The people of Orbost have decided to make a study of their own. This involves taking wandering anthropologists out for a night on the tiles and then back to the Red River Motel for a couple of skull bongs, a carton of UDL Drambuie and Dry and some tough love.

I know the sheila who's typing up the paper. 'How Anthropologists React under Severe Stress', I think it's called. It should be worth a read.

Western Australia

Motto	Load it on a jumbo, send it overseas
Faunal Emblem	African violet
Floral Emblem	~~Glossy Black Cockatoo~~, ~~Southern Bandicoot~~, ~~Koala~~, Labrador

Western Australia isn't really part of Australia. Yeah, I know, it looks like it's part of the vast brown continent of *Terra Australis* but the reality is, it was shoved across from Africa a couple of hundred years ago by long boat and sewn onto the Australian mainland by some very talented seamstresses who double stitched the thing into place along the South Australian and Northern Territory borders. They did very good work, too. Don't get me wrong, I'm not complaining about the work.

But that's why white South Africans like it so much when they get there. White South Africans feel right at home in Western Australia because it's actually part of Africa.

Sure the Jaapies whine that you can't get decent help in Western Australia. They moan that they can't find a decent gardener who'll pop down the diamond mines on his day off and have a good fossick around for them. They snarl at the waiter who's slavishly bringing them a few drinks and a sausage because he won't give them a free foot rub. But they still like the place a lot.

Western Australia: nourishing an insatiable world

Anyway, we're stuck with Western Australia now and it's right and proper that we move on and try and make the most of it.

The best thing is the bit of Africa that got dragged across to be slotted next to Australia seems to be one of the best bits of Africa. It's full of minerals and vitamins and is almost entirely Ebola free. After a particularly long session on the crème de cassis with Nigerian

Cardinal, Frank Arinze, I picked up a spot of Ebola. It was terrible. The worst gas I've ever had. I had to flush the thing right out of me with 1200 litres of crème de menthe. I farted like a Clydesdale for three days before I came good. But your chances of picking up a nasty case of Ebola in Western Australia are remote at worst.

Toxic Brian: I met him once – over breakfast, brunch, lunch, dinner and supper

Nowadays, Western Australia is the vast quarry of Australia and everyone over there is flat out digging it up and loading it all on burners to the Chinese. Some very smart people around the scene have made a quid out of it, too. And I'm happy to tell you that I am mates with them all. Everyone except Laurie Connell, who is brown bread now, but back when he was still drawing breath through the fetid cloud of a couple of packets of Viscount a day, he was a tremendous bloke to be around.

Laurie Connell was a great man and we spent many happy days at the races, punting like madmen. He had a real gift for the punt, too. Not only could he tell you the winner of a race, he could tell you if it was going to die within an hour or so of finishing its run, which was a tremendous help for me in putting my quadrellas together. He was a true visionary.

And Alan Bond can make money out of thin air. He's a very gifted bloke. Even after Bondy spent four years in the slammer for his role in the biggest corporate fraud in Australian history, the banks were falling over themselves to lend him money and they didn't seem to mind that he never paid it back.

I suppose it's about time I let bygones be bygones and accepted that Western Australia – the newcomers to the whole Australian caper – belong here as much of the rest of us do.

'TOXIC' BRIAN BURKE

JACK'S FACTS

Toxic Brian was a mate of mine until he became a person of interest in the Crime and Corruption Commission in Western Australia and I had to drop him like a 20-kilotonne atomic bomb over Hiroshima.

But back in the eighties we were very close. What a time Toxic Brian and I had then – zooming around the world in Bondy's zeppelin, punting like lunatics with Laurie Connell and all washed down with a bit of high-octane philately.

What sort of a nation have we become when we are judged by the blokes we bump into around the traps? Short of the nation taking out an apprehended violence order against Toxic Brian, prohibiting him from coming within 200 metres of any person within the Commonwealth of Australia, I don't know what the solution is.

Australian Capital Territory

Motto	Kill me. Somebody please kill me.
Faunal Emblem	Feral cats
Floral Emblem	Prickly pear

The Australian Capital Territory is the home of Canberra and is therefore the most awful place in the world.

After a bit of dithering on the part of our Founding Fathers, a pin was poked into a map in 1908 and the Yass/Canberra district was declared the site for Australia's national capital, thus spoiling a very nice sheep run once and for all.

In 1909, there was a nationwide SMS poll to decide which draughtsman's vision of the city looked best and a Yank by the name of Walter Burley Griffin won it hands down.

Griffin designed Canberra based on a series of enormous roundabouts. Today, the few tourists dim enough to travel there can be seen driving around and around on these, swearing angrily at one another while their children weep in the back seats.

Griffin decided to create the parliament as the centrepiece of Canberra and even went so far as to name it, rather hopefully, the 'Great Hall of the People'. And for a while that's what it was. Back then, you could casually stroll into Parliament House, have a counter lunch in the private members' dining room and, over a few schooners of crème de menthe, tell anybody from the prime minister down what was wrong with the country and how to bloody well fix it.

The Aga Khan and his missus. He hated Canberra almost as much as I do.

But those days are over. It had to happen. You know, the inexorable march of progress and all that. Now the new Parliament House has got 'Fuck Off' written all over it. If you're slender enough to squeeze past the bollards out the front, a bouncer will stick a finger up your date, on the off-chance that you're trying to smuggle in a few tabs of ecstasy to cheer the place up a bit. Aside from that, it's all become very impersonal.

The rest of Canberra has kicked on too. Back when I started out in the nation's capital, there was nowhere to take visiting dignitaries. Sure, you could take them to the bloody Art Gallery or to the War Museum but where would you take them for a few drinks and a lie-down with a ladyboy or two?

There weren't any restaurants to speak of either – none of the calibre I consider acceptable for international panjandrums. I remember back in the 1980s when the Aga Khan was in town doing a bit of business. The poor bastard hadn't eaten in two days. All I could do was take him for a drive to Guilfoyle's milk bar for a microwave chicken schwarma. He didn't say anything but I could tell he wasn't impressed.

It's gotten a lot better since. Nowadays there's a host of decent clubs and nightspots where you can take a visiting president or a United Nations wallah for a schooner and a swan and all you have to do is push the pissed pollies out of the road to get a good table.

With Australia's heavy investment in bureaucracy, Canberra has experienced a growth spurt in recent times. Urban planners have begun to tap their watches impatiently at Gough, Mal Fraser, Hawkie and little Johnnie Howard. The planners need to get their trammels out and create a few new suburbs and Gough and co are making it very difficult for them to come up with the names.

I suppose it will all get sorted out in time.

WALTER BURLEY GRIFFIN: KER-PLUNK GENIUS

The Chicago-born architect, town-planner and the man responsible for the travesty that is Canberra today also invented the game of Ker-Plunk.

Griffin became so obsessed with Ker-Plunk that his original drawings for the planned town of Griffith in south-western New South Wales included the provision of an enormous clear plastic tube in the middle of the town, thirty long, thin sticks and thirty-two marbles the size of beach balls.

While presenting his plans for the town to some New South Wales Government wallahs, Griffin broke into an eerie chant: 'Ker-Plunk is the game where you take your pick and pull a stick. If all the marbles fall, you lose it all! You're only sunk if they go . . . Ker-Plunk!'

As Griffin was the only person to have been interested enough to offer a plan for Griffith, a wary New South Wales Government was obliged to award him the contract.

The enormous Ker-Plunk structure was quietly and discreetly removed from the township shortly after Griffin's death in 1937.

Northern Territory

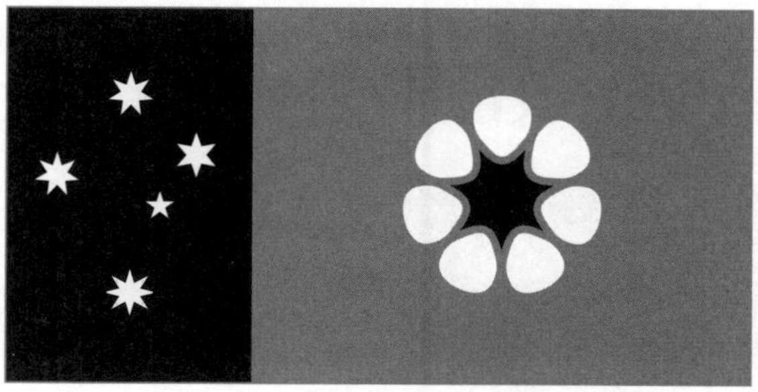

Motto	Get back, I've got a gun
Faunal Emblem	Angry loners
Floral Emblem	Nothing grows there

I've never been to Darwin and wouldn't go there unless there was a very big drink in it for me. I've made my mind up to avoid the place strictly on religious grounds. When you name a city after a bloke that tore the Book of Genesis to ribbons and pointed out many of God's shortcomings, there's always going to be trouble.

Subsequently, Darwin has had a couple of false starts, urban development wise. A bit of strafing from the Japanese during World War II saw off many of the more garish features of its neo-colonial architecture.

After the unannounced drop-ins from the Japanese, the people of Darwin reached for the cinder blocks and asbestos sheets and rebuilt in earnest. Just as he banged the last nail in the HardiPlank, the mayor of Darwin, Tiger Brennan, looked around and remarked, 'Geez, that wind's picked up.'

It was right back to the drawing board from there. It's as much a credit to their fortitude as it is clinical evidence of the delusional effects of alcohol that these people knuckled down and had another crack.

Confused about politics and not even sure if they're Australian or not, Territorians have decided not to decide in matters of statehood, preferring to get on the drink and watch the footy.

In 1998, Northern Territorians loaded up their pig dogs, their shotties and four slabs of Emu Bitter and headed off to town to smudge an inky thumb on the ballot paper in a referendum to determine if they were going to move up to the big league of statehood. It was either that or stay in a place that sounds like it was colonised by Inuits in the eighth century.

Unfortunately, the Territory was unable to find three sober men to act as scrutineers, so a resounding 'no' vote was recorded. The Territorians scratched their heads at first but then pronounced themselves pleased with the outcome and ordered a round of drinks.

They're in a bugger of a place, the Territorians, no doubt about it. Still, I love them to bits and would happily get on the piss with them at a moment's notice. Anywhere but Darwin.

The Japs attack Darwin and another urban redevelopment gets underway

Australian Antarctic Territory

Motto	Did someone leave the door open?
Faunal Emblem	Plankton
Floral Emblem	Bigger plankton

Australia owns a huge chunk of Antarctica; over six million square kilometres of frozen, desolate terrain that the rest of the world continues to eye off greedily. With Australia's military resources stretched to breaking point around the globe, the federal government has been forced to press-gang emperor penguins into service to protect Australia's interests south of the 60th parallel.

The alternative is to allow Australian scientists to look after the place and really, that's just asking for trouble. Having a bunch of Australian scientists running around, looking quizzical and poking their pipe-stems into things keeps them out of harm's way but they've never been any good in a stink.

Still, I can't help but think we're expecting too much from the penguin community. The penguins are staunch and ready to die for Australia but the only blues they've ever been involved in were against leopard seals and orcas and they've come off second best on all occasions. And they lack air support. The albatrosses give them buggery as it is.

The Antarctic in general and Mawson's Hut in particular need protecting. Douggie Mawson would be very fucking angry if he found out we'd given it up to the Chileans or, God forbid, the Norwegians. If the Norwegians moved in and turned it into a sauna and spa, I wouldn't be able to look at an old hundred-dollar note without a deep sense of shame, knowing I could have done something to stop it.

Heavily armed penguins maintain a constant vigil for signs of Chilean expansionism. But will it be enough?

Norfolk Island

Motto	My cousin has real purty hair.
Faunal Emblem	Bark and twigs
Floral Emblem	Colleen McCullough

Settled during Australia's 'tough on crime' stance in the early nineteenth century, the legacy of Norfolk Island's convict heritage sees its residents today proudly walking about the island with their cherished belongings stuffed up their dates.

After convicts declined very polite requests from residents to come back and help with a spot of gardening, Norfolk Island experienced a long period of isolation from the rest of the world. As the population dwindled, residents were forced to breed with the bottle-nosed dolphin, making their offspring excellent swimmers, but unable to represent Australia in the Olympics, as they become easily distracted if someone throws a ball into the pool.

Norfolk Islanders love Colleen McCullough and while away the hours creating images of the novelist from their own ear wax, like the one shown above

In 2002, Attorney-General Philip Ruddock legally excised Norfolk Island from Australia with an elegant stroke of a pen, in the continuing fight against people smugglers. Crafty New Zealanders now travel to Norfolk Island seeking refugee status, knowing full well that they will be shipped off to the United States where they can take that trip to Disneyland they've always wanted.

Cocos Island, Christmas Island, Ashmore Reef and Cartier Reef

Forget what the map says, you are not in Australia. Go away.

The Tragedy of the States

We should never have had the states. Every sane man and woman knows this. They should be abolished and the nation broken up into hundreds of small, autonomous collectives; each one with a barter economy and its own film industry, where everyone would exchange eggs, goats or screenplays with one another. Just like Tom and Barbara on *The Good Life*.

Each of these communities should be completely self-sufficient. Romania had a good crack at complete self-sufficiency before the brave Ceauşescu was brought down by the CIA. North Korea is still giving it a good go, despite the odd outbreak of bark-eating and cannibalism. It's not always easy, but everyone has a job. Half the country makes metal-tipped shoelaces, and the other half buys them. It's so fucking simple even an economist can understand it.

Know this: the push for national standards that followed Federation is a tragedy.

As I wrote in my book *Australia: A Big Fucking Disappointment* (which was launched by Bob Carr), New South Wales and Queensland and Victoria all had their own way of doing things before they federated.

I put this truth once to Geoffrey Blainey at one of those receptions for Australia's National Living Treasures that one is expected to attend from time to time. Blainey spat out his cocktail onion and spluttered, 'What about the rail gauge? Victoria and South Australia and Queensland all had different rail gauges! Think of the cost! Think of the inconvenience!'

'Aha!' I said, because I knew I had him. 'You think about the jobs that were lost! Back then, at the border, there was a little man employed to shake every passenger awake at 3 am and order them onto another train.'

'But—' Blainey was exasperated because he knew I was right. I pressed on.

'Another little man was employed to sell new tickets. Another to punch a hole in it. Another to check that the hole had been punched correctly. Another to inspect every lump of coal to ensure its coal-ishness, and so on.'

Blainey was on the ropes.

'All those men had jobs, Blainey. And with their wages they bought locally manufactured string, hand-cranked pasta machines and cat toys. Then the rails were standardised and their jobs disappeared. Proud men whose great-grandfathers had been ticket hole punchers and coal inspectors wept openly.'

Blainey made a move to escape to the toilet, but I caught his arm.

'And those men never received another paycheck. And they never bought the locally made pasta machines and cat toys, and the workers at those factories were let go. And they, in turn, never purchased locally made novelty telescopes. And that factory had to close too. And then the local disco ball factory. When they lost the hole punchers, they lost the disco balls as well. Do you see that now?'

I dared him to publicly debate me in North Korea in a month's time, and then I let him go. I showed up in Pyongyang, but he didn't. Which means I won the argument.

Prove I lie, Blainey.

CHAPTER FOUR

Local Government

There's Not a Drink in It, So Why Bother?

Local Government

I was elected alderman for a Gold Coast council a few years back. I only had a crack at it because I was trying to push through a rather delicate development approval on my beach house. All I wanted to do was put a carport in – above the mezzanine, right past the ballroom and the conservatory. The local punters swarmed all over my idea to have their bins collected daily and I won by a landslide. I got the carport knocked up the next Sunday morning, in anticipation.

The following Tuesday I marched off triumphantly to my first council meeting. You wouldn't believe it but I had to bring my own drinks. The whole thing was a shambles. My D.A. got knocked back, my pit bull was marked for execution and I was told I would incur a huge fine if I kept pumping my septic tank out into the Tweed River.

Some people don't understand what makes the world turn and these people almost invariably sit in local government. I told them all to get fucked; I walked out and haven't been back. A mob that plays God as badly as these clowns do just simply isn't worth my time.

CHAPTER FIVE

The Media

And What You Can Do to Stop It

The Media: A Short History

It was all Johannes Gutenberg's fault. Gutenberg invented movable type while toiling for years out of a lockup in an industrial estate in Mainz, Germany. In 1454, he knocked out copies of the Latin Vulgate translation of the Bible, some hardcore pornography and an EH Holden mechanics' manual that mystified the locals for years.

Not long afterwards, the first newspaper turned up on nature strips, hurled in the general direction of houses by careless paper boys. The communications revolution was underway.

It was at or around this time that the media got invented. Actually, it had been around for a while but it had always been a closed shop. Before Gutenberg, the church ran the media and made it clear it didn't much go for monks buttonholing the Pope to ask him a lot of impertinent questions about his sex life. And while illustrators worked hard, they could never keep up on the demand for the Hanseatic League's 'Ten Worst Dressed List'.

By the time Australia got invented, the media was already veering dangerously out of control. The media started the Spanish-American War in 1898. In New York, publishers geed up an anxious public with headlines like 'Spaniards Eat Your Babies' and 'Tapas is Fucked'. Since then the media has grown up heaps. In today's Australia, it exists in an almost perfect form. It's managed to streamline itself very efficiently, shedding useless journalists who ask too many questions for their own good, and narrowing the list of proprietors to an easy-to-remember list of three: News Ltd, Fairfax and the corpse of Kerry Packer.

The Print Media

Arse Paper for an Insatiable Nation

Print media in Australia is fabulous. The newspapers in Australia are of the finest quality. I find them all very absorbent but *The Age* is something I always like to keep on hand on the odd chance of coming down with amoebic dysentery. *The Daily Telegraph* comes next. The *Tele*'s lifestyle guide can mop up gallons of liquid excrement. And who could go past the *NT News* while in the grip of a bowel evacuation of bone-shuddering proportions?

Besides their wonderful spongy paper, Australian newspapers tend to throw the ink around in the right places, too. They're always right and I believe everything I read in them, with one or two exceptions.

Right and Wrong

Your right-wing media types often moan that they are under-represented in the media. They cite this erroneous information as proof that the media is a left-wing circus and their own voices are a plaintive cry from the cheap seats of the diaspora.

I'm here to tell you that's just plain wrong. Whenever I wipe my arse with a newspaper, I manage to leave a streak of shit on some right-wing columnist's head shot. The truth is they're all over the place.

Akkers, Windo and Paddy

Piers Akerman, Keith Windschuttle and Paddy McGuinness have been as ideologically mobile as a greyhound with an ultra-thin condom full of amphetamines up its date. As young men they were hardcore, sandal-wearing lefties, the kind who would harangue you in the uni bar about the fuckin' Sandinistas until you had to glass them with an empty schooner.

After they left uni, these pious little comrades ran away from Mao and Castro as fast as their fat little legs could carry them. Last time I looked they'd dashed past Franco and were gaining fast on Genghis Khan. The good news is that even though they've changed their minds about every principle they once held dear, they're still pretty certain they know what's best for you.

Gerard Henderson

It's just as well someone is keeping track of all this historical revisionism. And that someone is my old mate Gerard Henderson. Gerard works at the Sydney Institute – not dissimilar to the Pond's Institute as I understand it: a bunch of clowns in lab coats injecting chemicals into the eyeball of a rabbit. The only difference with Gerard's mob is that rabbits are push-polled afterwards.

Gerard keeps files on the foolish utterances of our political leaders and pundits. To date they take up several football fields' worth of real estate. Gerard himself has been extremely careful never to make wild predictions. In fact he's reluctant to concede anything about the past as well; he still won't acknowledge that the Boer War is over. He's too smart to be caught out on that one.

Gerard has the 'Grumpy but Loveable Conservative' market stitched up in this country, and he's stuck to the knitting for decades now. Only hours after his birth Gerard declared to his startled mother that he was pitching his tent with the conservatives from now on and, to his credit, he hasn't budged an inch.

Flinty

Let me be clear: everyone changes and grows with the passage of the years. Even my old mate David Flint, the former head of the Australian Broadcasting Authority and friend of Alan Jones. These days Flinty is an urbane chap, a dapper boulevardier who has mastered the art of the matching tie and handkerchief like no-one else in the country. You'd never think that back in the seventies, Flinty used to be a three-foot tall transsexual midget who made a living cleaning out the spittoons in a Saskatchewan brothel – and that's because it's not actually true. Flinty's a man's man and he wouldn't be caught dead cleaning out a spittoon.

The Left-Wing Commentariat

It's a sad fact that the well-meaning enthusiasts on the right have to live with cheap heckling from their nauseating left-wing counterparts: a bunch of snooty, up-themselves elitists who appear to be thrilled to bits that the war in Iraq is a failure.

These 'ner-nerni-nerni-ner-ner' types in the peanut gallery are demanding that Akerman, Greg Sheridan, Andrew Bolt, Miranda Devine, etc, should pause for a minute to question their own strident certainties and own up that they might not be right all of the time. Well here's a newsflash: they're not paid to be right. They're paid to be certain. Which is why, comrade, *your* opinion column lies buried under the ads for compost bins in *Green Left Weekly* and Piers is on the op-ed page of the *Telegraph*. Right or wrong on Iraq? Who gives a shit?

Happily, most of these rabid pinkos have been forced out of the media. Unable to bear the taunt from the right, 'If you don't like it, why don't you go and live in Russia?', many did, and were slaughtered en masse for failing to reach the state-determined turnip yield.

The so-called left-wing intelligentsia always hated John Howard because he wanted to drag the country back to the fifties. They, on the other hand, want to drag us back to the seventies, which is an advance of a good two decades or so. This is why they're called 'progressives'.

The truth is that these types are loaded up with a weird kind of fetishistic, national self-loathing. This makes them interesting as occasional sexual partners, but then the post-coital conversation would send you searching for the nearest brick wall to casually dash your brains out.

Phillip Adams

Now when I speak of lefty columnists, the chief flag waver is Phil. Firstly let me say this: Phillip Adams is a terrific bloke. I've spent many weekends with the man on his farm in Scone, sleeping overnight in a spare Egyptian sarcophagus he keeps in the guesthouse. He's a great Australian.

But Phillip has a terrible secret. He'll bloody kill me for revealing this, but Phillip's been writing columns for nearly four decades now; we know what he thinks already about everything. That's why he's outsourced his weekly column to Mumbai, where a factory full of Indian kiddies cut and paste together bits from his previous work and then fax it to *The Australian*.

This is Phillip Adams, not Santa: confusing the two could ruin your entire Christmas

How to Survive as a Newspaper Columnist

Being a columnist is easy. Like most things, getting the gig is always the hard part. I've always found getting a managing editor comatose on the drink and then lining him up with a Romanian stripper for the evening generally greases the wheels in a most satisfactory manner.

The thing about being a columnist is that once you're in and you see your dial beaming back at you from the op-ed pages, you can't be shifted with a crowbar and a bucket of axle grease. You're there for life and nothing short of the Rapture will see you off.

Still, writing thousands of words every week can become a chore. Having an opinion is the easy part. Opinions are like arseholes – everyone's got one. But getting the words down on the page to deadline can be a bit stressful, especially if you've spent the last week in a Kowloon brothel on an opium binge.

The old salts around the traps can show you a way around the problem. Experienced columnists know the short cuts. They hate the very thought of sitting down hammering their fingers into bloodied nubs on a keyboard all day. After all, it's a serious distraction from the important business of drunken five-hour lunches.

Here's a few tips from the masters on how to avoid the horrible panic of the blank page and get that copy fired off to a grateful editor on time, every time.

Alan 'Scissorhands' Ramsey (*The Sydney Morning Herald*)

The Australian print media's ultimate curmudgeon, Scissorhands has been around the caper for longer than anyone can remember. He was banging away about Menzies on an Olivetti typewriter when Laurie 'Jabba the Hutt' Oakes was eating crayons and pissing in a sandpit. What Scissorhands doesn't know about the caper isn't worth knowing.

Step one: Quickly knock up an introduction, laced with confected outrage. Something like:

Just when you think things couldn't get any worse, the [insert name of government here] pulls a stunt so despicable and vile that you vomit all over yourself.

Step two: Find a murky and meaningless tract from Hansard. It doesn't matter what it's about. A diatribe from a pollie who has leapt to his or her feet in parliament, bemoaning the appalling state of poultry farming in the Simpson Desert will do nicely.

Step three: Ctrl C

Step four: Ctrl V

Step five: Write a short concluding paragraph. This one always works well:

The [insert name of government here], eh? What a pack of bastards.

Step six: File copy and wait for the cheque to arrive in the mail.

Alan Belford Jones (formerly of *The Sun-Herald*)

Jonesy's a big reader. He's got a ton of books from the airport in his bookcase just to prove it. And Jonesy figures no-one understands international relations better than Frederick Forsyth. So what if Forsyth's in the business of knocking up racy novels rather than doing the hard yards of international diplomacy and policy development? Forsyth and others of his ilk have knocked up hundreds of thousands of very usable words based on international scenarios where goodies lurch around from crisis to crisis and bad guys laugh maniacally while stroking furry cats. This is always a help for columnists who only understand the world in simple black and white terms rather than the chaotic, amoral, greyish hue it really is.

Step one: Find an obscure tome written by Forsyth or Tom Clancy or Colin Forbes. Almost anyone will do.

Step two: Highlight a few paragraphs and fling it at your personal assistant, demanding that she type them up, pronto.

Step three: Receive the copy and attach a handwritten letter to the editor, effusive in praise.

Step four: Knock up a quick correction and apology for the previous week's column to avoid a monstrous defamation payout.

Step five: Head off to coach a rugby league team. Badly.

Andrew Bolt (*Herald Sun*)

Young Bolty is still in short pants compared with Scissorhands and Jonesy, but he's still got a few important tips to offer the young punter who wants to get into the column writing caper. Bolty's work provides a standout example of one of the most important aspects of a column writer's art: never let the facts get in the way of a good yarn.

Take climate change, for instance. Now there's a heavy body of science, plucked from a substantial group of boffins in lab coats playing around with test tubes who reckon Planet Earth may be in for a bit of a rough ride in the near future.

Bolty isn't a scientist, of course. He's flat out putting petrol in his car. But the concept of global warming is repellent to him because a) he didn't think of it first and b) it contradicts his long-held view that the world will end at the hands of Islamo-fascist terrorists, sooner rather than later.

Even a gifted polemicist like Bolt would struggle to create a cogent, coherent, compelling argument refuting climate change. Research will be crucial here and it's important to do as little as possible.

Step one: Receive copies of scientific reports from such august bodies as the World Meteorological Organization and the United Nations Environment Programme and hurl them in the bin.

Step two: Conduct internet-based research. Google the words 'al-Qaeda', 'Kyoto Agreement' and 'Andrew Bolt'. Find nothing of use.

Step three: Interview a beautician from Moonee Ponds who thinks global warming is a crock of shit and can't understand what all the fuss is about.
NB: You can have a haircut at the same time.

Step four: Quote beautician at length. Then skew your argument to take in all manner of irrelevant facts and sundry apocrypha. Conclude by saying that global warming is an elegant fraud perpetrated on the world by Islamic extremists.

Step five: Type in the happy words 'column ends' and pop off to the pub.

Good Heads for Radio

In Australia, your crystal set screams at you in one of two ways: with god-awful hits from the seventies or strident jocks shoving their ghastly opinions down your throat.

If you're a coffin-dodger, you listen to Jonesy. If you're in the autumn years, it's Kyle Sandilands tormenting prostitutes. If you're a kiddie, you've got your head stuck in an iPod and couldn't give a fuck about the radio.

They don't go for advertising at the ABC although they do a nice little turn in promoting themselves. The ABC transmits gigahertz of sound waves every day in the hope that someone is listening. There's News Radio which will fill you in on events from two days ago on a fifteen-minute loop. Then there's ABC FM, but the only people who tune in are ham radio operators from the Czech Republic.

Ultimately, I wouldn't give it the time of day. Radio broadcasting is no way to make a living in my opinion, Johnnie Tapp excepted.

My Mate Jonesy

In May 2004, Jack the Insider delivered this strident oration in defence of Alan Jones and David Flint to a motley collection of slavering ABC journalists outside the Australian Industrial Relations Commission in Sydney.

My friends . . .

I am a friend of Alan Jones. I am not afraid of saying that here or anywhere else. He is a terrific bloke. Like me, he is a lover of sports and sportsmen and I am proud to say that he and I have spent many happy hours together in the crawl space of his home keeping a fatherly eye, through the heating vents, on the young athletes bunking in there.

Jonesy is a man's man but he's also a sensitive bloke and a bloke sensitive to the needs of other blokes. He's not afraid to front a man he's never met before in the street or indeed in a public convenience and offer him a few dollars and a kind word.

Very unfairly in my opinion, Jonesy got punted from the school. Of course Jonesy misses the school boys, but he has since turned to the radio waves and extended the love shown to that lucky group of students to a city that had forgotten the meaning of media totalitarianism.

My good mate David Flint was in inextricable piles of excrement – up to his fuckin' eye teeth in shit shovelled in his general direction by a handful of pinko ABC journalists just because he had the good sense to call Alan Jones his mate.

Flinty and I have one thing in common. Actually several things, if truth be known. We both hanker for the grand days of the Plantagenets, when kings were gods and peasants were garroted in their thousands for failing to accept their lot, get on with their filth-encrusted existences and put their kids down the mines. Flinty and I agree – it's the monarchy for us and the very thought of an elected Australian-born clown as the head of state causes us to vomit bile out of our nostrils in great steaming green streams.

Flinty and I are also very keen on Jesus and believe fans of other messianic figures are for the off, to be burned in hell for all eternity. He and I regularly swap the ceremonial duties of marching through Bondi with a 300-kilogram crucifix strapped to our backs at Easter time. I did it last year and Flinty did it this year on Good Friday. Just to make sure he was aware of the full spiritual significance of what he was doing, I slammed a few roofing nails into his hands and feet with a ballpein hammer. Christ, Flinty bled bucketloads but he did not demur and kept up a stiff walking pace despite the obvious handicap of having a couple of hundredweight of asphalt impaled to the soles of his feet. He's a fuckin' pro, Flinty, you've got to give him that. He just won't say no to a challenge.

But the one thing we really have in common is that we are both appointed by the Crown. And as such we are entitled to tell the general populace to get well and truly fucked when they have the cheek to tell us how we can and can't earn a quid and who we can and can't write fawning letters to.

But recent scurrilous attempts to shitcan Flinty in the media appear to have softened his resolve. Flinty and I were at Dapto just last week, watching a few dishies goin' around. He loves the lickers, Flinty, but last Monday he looked careworn and distracted. After watching him plonk his hard-earned on a crazy multiple trifecta made up of four drug-fucked no-hopers, I pulled him up, slapped him hard across the face and asked him what the fuck was going on.

He sobbed and told me that the media had him by the balls. He was fucked, he blubbered, and had nowhere to hide. With a deep sense of resignation he told me he would have to tender his resignation. No! I told him, don't take any shit from the media – stand tall, head up, chin out. Didn't they realise that he was at the helm of one of this country's most piss-weak statutory authorities? The media, I told him, can get fucked.

After all these are the Howard years. And when you're appointed by the Crown, you can tell whoever you like to get fucked, even Howard himself. The only person you need to stay cosy with is Jonesy. Jonesy could hate for Australia and will cross George Street on a Friday night to go you. I told Flinty of the time when, in a moment of rash thoughtlessness, I reminded Jonesy of that shit-awful talkback TV show he did on Channel Ten in the eighties. The next thing I knew I was bundled into the back of a divvy van and was charged with the disappearance of the Beaumont children. The charges were later dropped after I told police that I'd been attending to duties for Victorian premier Sir Henry Bolte at the time the kids vanished, and my story checked out. But I learned my lesson and Flinty would have to learn his.

And so it was with a profound sense of relief that I observed Flinty had very sensibly pulled his head in and just late last week looked down the barrel of an ABC TV camera and strongly urged the nation to get fucked.

Now we know that the Howard years have not been kind to the youth of the nation. While some children are locked up for the crime of lobbing on the North West Cape in a leaky boat, others have to resign themselves to being sexually assaulted by second-rate teachers with no flair for broadcasting. But for the rest of us, as my mate Jonesy will tell you, the Howard years are this country's golden age; a time where Jonesy stands astride the nation, like a colossus, answerable to no-one.

And if you don't like it, well, you can get fucked.

KEEPING THE DREAM ALIVE

JACK'S FACTS

John Laws dominated his morning timeslot for decades and no wonder. Lawsy had a little trick he'd perform every day that delivered him a significant psychological edge over the gutless parasite sitting in the interview chair. Every morning before going on air, the great man would simply take his pants off. After removing his Amco V-Knees with the big belt buckle, he'd carefully drape them over the arm of a concrete lawn jockey before grabbing the golden microphone with both hands and bellowing, 'Hello world!'

John Laws: man of the people

Australian Telly – Now Without Colour

In the olden days you could watch telly and see Muhammad Ali and Joe Frazier beat each other senseless, followed by Mannix kicking some crims to death and wind up a top night's entertainment with *Pot Black* – all in wondrous black and white. The moment we went to colour, something terrible happened. There's been nothing of interest on the telly since.

Channel Seven

Channel Seven now runs over six hours of news and current events each day, just to give all the expats from Nine something to do. But none of it is hard news. It's mostly dogs that bark in tune to music and beer-drinking sheep squeezed in between the game shows.

Seven's flagship show used to be *Today Tonight*. Every weeknight at 6.30 the champion of Australian values and scourge of fat kiddies, Filipino tradesmen and road hoons clears its throat and gives us the good oil on fat pills. It's just a pity Naomi Robson got the flick. She was a good sort – a lot of fun to spend a night on the tiles with and what's more, she knew how to put fat people in their place.

These days the Seven Network's top show is *Sunrise*, hosted by Mel and Kochie and that grinning boy-man Grant Denyer.* *Sunrise* is a terrific place to showcase your new book/film/tax reform project/threat to incinerate the Western infidel. The only problem is you've got to be sober and coherent at 6 am. My advice is fly to London and do it from there. They're onto their second coffee but you're onto your second cask of Bold Red. The words will flow that much easier, I promise you.

Channel Nine

The Nine Network, a once-great institution, used to love to break prime ministers on a rack, tear off bits of bleeding meat and throw them to the Australian public. Paul Keating knew he was finished in 1996 when Kerry Packer casually mentioned that John Howard would make a cracker of a PM on *A Current Affair*. Likewise, Little Johnnie thought he was cactus when Big Kezza's reanimated corpse was wheeled out to announce that he had put a lazy five hundred grand on the Ruddster in 2007 at good odds. But lately, things have been on the slide for Nine. For decades the network was able to maintain its supremacy with a simple winning formula:

1. Put Australian cricketers in canary yellow outfits.

2. Hire a sheila who looks like a stripper and get her to read the finance report.

3. Give Eddie McGuire a gig, but never, ever let him near the family business.

---

* It's a little known fact that Grant Denyer is actually a mandrill. The story I heard is that Denyer showed up for a read-through one day, and – despite being a mandrill – he astonished the Seven bigwigs with his smooth delivery. They gave him a gig at once. The Seven makeover team shaved him down, painted his bright vermilion arse a more acceptable puce and taught him to drive a car. He's been going gangbusters ever since, although the sphincters of Seven Network heavies tighten involuntarily every time Denyer shuns the autocue and goes into an impromptu rant. They've got no-one but themselves to blame. Like most monkeys, it's all about the training.

Sadly, since the demise of Big Kezza, the last two of these precepts have been completely ignored by clueless carpet strollers. Consequently viewers have turned to other networks for their daily injection of fear, hatred and vague titillation. Nine is no longer able to inspire stark terror. It used to be said: when Nine says you're fucked, you're fucked. These days, when Nine says you're fucked, odds are you're a co-host of the *Today* show.

Eddie McGuire toiled hard at the Nine cafeteria: his shit sandwiches became the most popular item on the menu

Channel Ten

Watching Ten News is like getting a report from your demented uncle – the guy who sits around in his underpants, gesticulating wildly, babbling about a bunch of guys, one of whom had a beard and looked really nasty, who had a car crash or a pub fight or got stuck in a storm-water drain. Or something.

Ten runs its evening news at 5 pm as a service for the perpetually stoned. Somehow they're able to run a one-hour bulletin with only three minutes of news; the rest is filled with sport and weather.

Political reports generally take up a full thirty seconds, leaving plenty of time for stories about rodeo chimpanzees and cats that wander back home after leaping out of the family car in the Simpson Desert.

Ten's managers have a knack for containing costs. Every time there's a 'gay' story they run the same footage of poofs in golden shorts from a Mardi Gras that was shot twenty years ago. It's a terrific way to enhance shareholder value.

Big Brother isn't the big earner it used to be for the network: mainly because, after seven years, they're running out of irritating bogans. They've been reduced to sending Kyle Sandilands into the house for chrissakes.

But the future looks bright for Ten as emerging political analysts and insiders, Andrew G and James Mathison, look set to put the pads on and do the hard work out in the middle, politically speaking, for the network in future.

SBS

SBS proudly runs contrary to its charter. The Australia-wide multicultural broadcaster is supposed to run programs that are a) multicultural and b) multilingual. Besides the odd French film, if you've got a hankering to watch the telly in languages other than English, you'll have to wait until 1.30 in the morning for *The Storm Rages Twice*, a Lebanese soapie which, I concede, has its moments.

Fortunately SBS more than makes up for the egregious breach of its charter by hiring newsreaders whose pronunciation of anything foreign is tortured to the point where you just wish they'd die already.

I once saw Stan Grant dislocate his tongue while trying to get his gob around the five syllables of South African President Thabo Mbeki's name. I thought that poor bastard Grant was trying to spit out 'pneumonoultramicroscopicsilicovolcanoconiosis'. He got halfway through and his eyes drifted into the back of his head. When he hit the deck hard, I knew he was in big trouble.

Thankfully, the Howard Government had allowed SBS to run ads by then, so we were spared the grisly sight of Stan Grant contorting on the ground. For once the publicly funded ads promoting domestic violence were a welcome relief.

When they cut back to the newsroom, Grant was gone and Lee Lin Chin had taken over and I must say the change was for the better.

I am more concerned about what's happening with Mary Kostakidis. I'm told SBS have taken a page or two out of the Eddie McGuire management playbook and got her eating shit sandwiches all day long. It's a disgrace. I've always had a deep, primal love for Mary. She's a Greek girl of course but that's still no reason to stick it to her in the arse.

The Canberra Press Gallery

Remember Medicare Gold? Marky Mark Latham's offer of free hospital care for the over-seventies? These days, to a man, the Canberra press gallery holds it up as the Leyland P76 of policy. A laughable dud. Everyone knows that.

Last month I had a quick flick through some newspapers from the 2004 campaign that happened to be lining the bottom of my nanna's budgie cage. Back then these eye-rolling idiots were hailing Medicare Gold as 'Latham's Masterstroke!' or 'Latham's Bold Bid for Power'. Laura Tingle called the thing a 'politically devastating policy idea'. Two weeks after the election she was on *Lateline* saying she always knew it was as useful as an ashtray on a motorbike.

Matty Price at *The Australian* likes to treat all policy failures with disdain, like an embarrassing fashion mistake: like, what were you thinking, girl? These days Pricey reckons that he always knew that Mad Mark was a demented lunatic. Pricey shakes his head in sorrow and says that Mark's great blunder was his troops-home-from-Iraq-by-Christmas pledge. We always knew that. But thumbing through those birdshit-stained copies of the *Oz* from a few years ago, I read that Matt thought Iraq would win the election for Mad Mark.

I've got nothing against a bit of crystal ball gazing. The racing industry is founded on it after all. What shits me to tears is when these pundits make a call, then pretend they didn't. And then say they always knew otherwise.

Up to Our Nuts in Blood and Guts

Every day we're confronted by images of death and misery on the streets of Baghdad. The liberal media seem to think that the more blood and carnage they show, the more people will be put off by war.

According to a wholly specious report that I glanced at briefly while spending several hours in quiet contemplation in the newsroom toilet, the contrary may well be the case. All that death can be very life-affirming. The more bloodstained body parts we see strewn about the streets of Sadr City and elsewhere in that worthless country, the more we believe that the coalition is on a winner. Iraqis are dying for a bit of democracy and it's an impressive thing to witness from the safety of our homes.

I'm sick and tired of these pinko moon-bats and their hand wringing. I mean what are they saying, that this type of bloodletting and human misery on our television screens is going to terrify young Australian kids while they're digesting their hoof-and-eyelid steaks and oven-fried chips?

These are Australian kiddies and they love it. If anything they'll get the smell of blood and human entrails wafting out from their TV sets and up their nostrils and feel the sudden uncontrollable urge to enlist with the ADF and set to work on the next Islamo-fascist nation to upset my acute sense of outrage.

The war with Saddam's Iraq lasted just weeks. The ensuing clean-up operations have taken a touch longer than expected. But during this important mopping-up phase, it is crucial that the youth of Australia witness up close every bit of blood-splattered footage. If nothing else, it's a salient reminder to Australian kids: clean up your rooms, or you'll have an M1 Abrams tank up your arse.

So I say to the youth of Australia: ignore the plaintive whimpering of the Marxist-Leninist baby boomers. Remember war is just like it is on your PlayStation, only you get cooler weapons. Turn on Fox News and get a good eyeful of it. Get into the feel, the atmosphere, the oeuvre of war.

The war to give Arabs the gift of democracy began in the eleventh century when Pope Urban II's army, led by Godfrey Bouillon, bravely massacred the residents of Jerusalem after they refused to register for the vote.

This war will go on for a millennium or two more yet. It's time to put your hand in the air. It's time to choose your side.

And if you're not on my side – the democracy-loving warmongers, urgers and war profiteers – you may as well plonk a pink carnation down the business end of an M16, held firmly in the hands of an angry marine. Just be careful it doesn't go off in your face and you end up on the telly.

The ABC – I Wouldn't Give You Eight Cents for It

JACK: Richard, pop down to the licensed grocers for me and get me a packet of Viscount and a litre of formaldehyde, son.

RICHARD: You've got a full bottle there and a carton of smokes in your top pocket, Jack . . .

JACK: Richard, I need to talk about the AB fuckin' C and I can't have you in the room while I'm doing it. So fuck off, son.

(Jack waits for the door to close before he draws heavily on a Viscount.)

The national broadcaster, friend, companion of the bush and twisted left-wing propagandist, the AB fuckin' C, continues to perform an outstanding community service in areas where it has no business sticking its gigantic, Stalinist nose.

With the demise of compulsory student unionism, it was obvious that the Australian Labor Party would soon struggle to recruit candidates with a solid background in pointless public policy and a finely tuned ability to stab their colleagues in the back.

Thankfully, the AB fuckin' C has taken up the slack and has now produced a fine crop of candidates who've renounced the national broadcaster, taken the superannuation and headed off to join up with Labor for a gig in parliament.

AB fuckin' C TV continues to lead the commercial networks in innovative programming, pumping out Carry On movies and cack-handed reality shows to a grateful public. The ABC charter stresses the need for local content on the telly and it manages to achieve this with low-rent programs for kiddies and broadcasting Tony Jones asleep at his home between the hours of 4 am and 6 am every day.

The AB fuckin' C aims squarely at the middle: middle class, middle brow, middle-aged and mediocre. They've got the antique-collecting, Ford Festiva–driving market stitched up. The rest of us who aren't into netball can get fucked.

Those on the right think the whole organisation should be flogged to a private equity consortium led by Macquarie Bank and relentlessly hived off in a series of diminishing chunks at garage sales until nothing remains.

I'm not averse to making a quid out of privatising the ABC. Trouble is, I wouldn't give you eight cents for it.

JACK: *(Beckons to Richard.)* Righto, son. You can come back in now.

Problem Identified

God-Awful Programming on ABC TV – Wednesday 27 March

6.00: Children's Programs (G) Four hours of low-rent, cheapjack entertainment that your children scream along to every morning. If you attempt to turn the television off or tinker with the volume, your kids will go you with a Phillips head screwdriver.

10.00: Educational Programs

Why Trees Are Cool (G) 2. Because They Just Are

Genetics. An Introduction (G) 4. Just Exactly Who Was John Merrick's Mum?

Blame It All On Howard . . . (G) Program which helpfully points out that children's lives are utterly without hope and that John Howard is solely to blame for the ongoing social tragedy. Hosted by Maxine McKew.

12.00: Midday News (MA, Rpt)) All the news from yesterday because the producer got into work three hours late with a hangover and doesn't give a fuck any more.

12.30: Screwin' the Menu (G, Rpt) Appalling and pointless cooking-show-come-holiday-magazine, featuring two young idiots on an all-expenses-paid trip around Australia who are so busy having fun that they make complete arses of themselves in the kitchen. This week, burned scallops on a lumpy celeriac mash are hurled into a bin.

1.00: National Press Club Address – Kevin Andrews (MA) The gnarled Howard Government veteran astonishes journalists by producing a yellow budgerigar which he strokes and coos to, in an effort to avoid scrutiny of his gormless performance as Minister for Industrial Relations and Minister for Immigration.

2.00: Parliament Question Time – House of Reps (MA) Politicians roused from their slumber stagger to their feet and ask puerile questions of the government. The government tells them to shut up and fuck off, which they do, after the Speaker threatens to have their eyes out with a stick.

3.00: Kids' TV (G, Rpt) The same crap that ran less than five hours ago on a seemingly infinite, drearily repetitive loop. Children, some as young as three, seem strangely aware that someone is taking the piss but their minds are already so addled by television that they barely notice.

6.00: A Day in the Life of a Mosquito (G, Rpt) Wildlife documentary. Using a tiny camera strapped to the head of a mosquito, we follow the insect as it hunkers down to suck the blood from an unidentified human arse, leaving Ross River fever and encephalitis as a parting gift before moving on to kill some children.

7.00: Evening News (MA) Joyless procession of misfortune and violence, made more palatable by being read by a woman in a bright floral jacket.

7.30: 7.30 Report (MA) Current affairs program. Tonight Kerry O'Brien interviews the prime minister. Kerry soon realises he's inadvertently delivered more than two hundred thousand votes to the beleaguered national leader by calling him 'a lying, coffin-dodging rodent' under his breath.

8.00: Shit Brit Sit-Com Compendium: It Ain't Half Hot, Mum On the Buses (PG, Rpt) Stan and Jack smuggle a thermonuclear device on the Number 43 bus, crowded with an army entertainment platoon fresh from the Malay Insurrection, unaware that Blakey has the trigger for the bomb and will detonate it at the Charing Cross Road, ending their vile mockery once and for all.

8.30: Spicks and Specks of Entertainment (PG) Comedian Adam Hills tries to keep publicity-starved stand-up comics at bay while attempting to host a game show. Tonight Mikey Robins interrupts Peter Helliar, forcing Helliar to stand up and walk around, shouting, before tipping a glass of water on himself. Robins counters by dropping his daks and doing the bulldog.

9.00: The Chaser's War on Comedy (M) Tired undergraduate schlock. Tonight Chas Licciardello masturbates into some ham, Chris Taylor kicks a horse to death at Warwick Farm and Andrew Hansen breaches a Supreme Court order that he never, ever sing on television again.

9.15: Media Botch (G) Unwatchable and pointless examination of the media by a prissy host who's been to one Walkley Award night too many. Tonight the editor of *Caravan Monthly* is ruthlessly tormented over his appalling use of apostrophes.

10.00: Your Say (M, Drug ref) Bowing to its charter, the ABC throws the airwaves open to the handful of viewers who remain watching. Tonight an Adelaide man in a stained bathrobe points an accusing finger at Australia's media cabal for ignoring his screenplay about bird flu Armageddon in Antarctica, while smoking a bong.

10.30: Lateline (MA) Current affairs program hosted by Tony Jones. Tonight an expose on reckless state government spending in health care that somehow sheets the blame home to John Howard.

11.00: Arts Review (X) A panel of sneering know-it-alls trade smug observations on cultural events in the past week, reflecting finally and sadly that no-one is watching and never will.

11.30: How Beige Was My Jacket (MA, Rpt) Period drama series set in the 1970s based on the life of a young working-class man from Leeds who aims to make it in the fashion industry. Tonight Adrian tells his father that he wants to become a fashion designer and is savagely beaten for his trouble. Final.

12.30: Movie: *Abbott and Costello Meet Josef Mengele* (1942 b/w, PG, Rpt) Hilarity ensues when Nazi villain Josef Mengele mistakes Bud Abbott and Lou Costello for twins. Stars John Wayne as Josef Mengele.

2.30: Movie: *Carry On Up The Spahn Ranch* (1974, MA, Rpt) Sid James stars as Charles Manson in this incredibly tasteless romp based on the Manson family murders. Under Sid's psychotic spell, Hattie Jacques, Joan Sims and Barbara Windsor break into Sharon Tate's house and commence an appalling, murderous rampage with Charles Hawtrey in tow, loudly exclaiming, 'Well, I never.'

Problem Solved

Jack the Insider's Guide to ABC TV Programming – Wednesday 27 March

6.00: Slap or Treat (G) Hyperactive children are taunted by a man wearing a bunny suit. One by one the mewling delinquents step forth and meet the bunny to be offered a chocolate surprise or an ear-ringing slap across the face from the bunny's huge, unforgiving hand.

7.30: Chainsaw Juggling (G) Incredibly irresponsible show in which children are encouraged to go into the garage, collect sharp, dangerous tools, hurl them into the air and attempt to catch them.

10.00: Educational Programs

How to Make a Halfway Decent Mint Julep (MA, CL, AC) Jack the Insider demands teenagers fix him a fucking drink already.

You're Out on Your Arse (MA) Jack the Insider tells teenagers that the education system has nothing left to offer them.

Get a Job! (MA, Violence, Adult Themes) Jack the Insider threatens teenagers with a stick, prodding them in the direction of the Centrelink office.

12.00: Chimp News (G) All the breaking news read by a chimpanzee in a waistcoat, smoking a cigar.

12.30: Shit Comedy Hour of Atonement (PG) Australia's least funny stand-up comedians are filmed performing acts of community service which in some small way make up for the hours of unspeakably joyless patter they've subjected us all to. This week Elliot Goblet picks up used syringes in Redfern with his teeth.

1.30: Pet Detention (G) Game show for pet owners. The winners receive ABC gift certificates. The losers have their pets incarcerated at Villawood Detention Centre while gormless Immigration Department officials determine their fate over the next five years.

2.00: The Bill (G) Feeling increasingly typecast as do-gooders, the gang from Sun Hill smoke crystal meth and head off on a three-day crime spree, committing numerous acts of riot and affray as well as an act of gross indecency on a duck that PC Tony Stamp thought was 'kinda cute'.

3.00: Kids' TV

Poo Piss Bum (M, CL) Naughty preschool children sitting in a sandbox, giggling and swearing.

We're Going Down! (G) Black box flight recordings from doomed aircraft, comically re-enacted by B1 and B2.

The Flatulents (G) Inexplicable children's program, featuring the flailing, farting duo dressed in harlequin outfits. This week: A Night at the Opera.

5.00: Angry Teenaged Loner Hour (MA, Violence) Morose, alienated teenagers speak of the utter pointlessness of life, how much they hate their parents, teachers and peers, and how they plan to get even with everyone one day, while cleaning guns and casually popping pimples on their foreheads.

6.00: Lodge Botherers (X) Cartoonist Warren Brown showcases the bizarre sexual peccadilloes of Australia's prime ministers. This week, Joe Lyons's disturbing predilection for infantilism is examined in excruciating detail.

7.00: News (MA) A grim post-mortem of war, death, poverty and unspeakable human misery, ending with a story about a cat that does the ironing which somehow makes it all seem worthwhile.

7.30: Knock an Orang Unconscious (G) Game show in which contestants are encouraged to march up and king-hit Taronga Zoo resident Jimmy the orangutan.

8.00: DT Dentist (G) Gripping fly-on-the-wall real-life drama in which an alcoholic dentist, suffering from delirium tremens, treats terrified patients to torturous extractions and seemingly endless root canal work with a drill he's forgotten to sterilise.

8.30: Celebrity Chef Meltdown (MA, CL, Violence) Everyone's favourite chef, Jamie Oliver, breaks down and admits he despises humanity and would happily poison every single one of us, if he had the chance.

9.30: Into Coursing (G) All the news from the world of greyhound racing, read by a cute sheila who is having her first run on the airwaves and is now deeply indebted to Jack in a very, very big way.

10.00: Virtual Drinking Buddy (MA, CL, AC) Jack the Insider sits down at a table and polishes off thirty-eight schooners of crème de menthe while staring directly down the barrel of the camera and telling increasingly lurid and obscene stories of his days in the army.

12.00: Australia's Funniest Bridge Collapses (G) Amateur video shot around the country, screened in an interminable loop to the accompaniment of music played by a single kazoo.

2.00: White Noise and Static (MA, Violence) Jack falls asleep on the couch with a Viscount dangling precariously from his gob.

Your Guide to Punching with the Media Heavyweights

WHAT'S THIS GUY'S NAME AGAIN? Y'KNOW, THINGO *aka Claude Rains*

Rating 

Comments: A Google search returned no results.

Watch out for: A desperate attempt to turn his fortunes around by conducting another tedious interview with Nicole Kidman. This will lead to him finishing his media career doing ads for the insurance industry.

KERRY *aka Red Kerry*

Rating 

Comments: A former ALP staffer who tries valiantly to show his political even-handedness but sadly always fails.

Watch out for: Red Kerry toning down the bile after he is told that every time he buttonholes John Howard in an interview, Howard picks up two points in the polls.

LAURIE *aka Jabba the Hutt*

Rating 

Comments: The doyen of all political journalists. Having been in the caper so long, he is distrusted and despised by all pollies regardless of their persuasion. Defied medical science by actually gaining weight after having his stomach stapled.

Watch out for: Keep your hands and feet well away from his mouth when he's eating, which is most of the time.

TONY JONES *aka Kerry Lite*

Rating 

Comments: Terrified of confrontation and timid in a blue, Jones is the interviewer pollies clamour for when they're in a spot of bother.

Watch out for: Frustrated with his nice guy image, Tony decides to ratchet up the aggro during an interview with Bindi Irwin and cops a right flogging.

LEE LIN CHIN *aka The Pipecleaner*

Rating

Comments: Kevin Rudd's newsreader of choice. Painfully thin and given to protracted and painful pronunciations of any word or term vaguely foreign.

Watch out for: Lee Lin Chin experiencing career-ending lockjaw while trying to read 'President Mahmoud Ahmadinejad' off the autocue.

THAT NICE GIRL WHO REPLACED NAOMI ROBSON *aka Anna Coren*

Rating

Comments: Nowhere near as much fun to spend a night out on the tiles with as Naomi Robson, but still, you know, kind of nice.

Watch out for: Thinks journalists live by a code of ethics. Fortunately, none work on her program.

KOCHIE AND MEL *aka The 'B' Team*

Rating

Comments: Light, fluffy and vaguely annoying yet unafraid to ask the hard questions as long as it doesn't clash with any commitments they've made to their advertisers.

Watch out for: Kochie looking for blood during the Powerade Political Hot Spot.

ANDREW G AND JAMES MATHISON *aka The 'A' Team*

Rating

Comments: The up-and-comers. The savvy political and cultural pathologists of tomorrow today. Hair to die for.

Watch out for: A hiccup in an otherwise faultless career when Andrew confuses the *Big Brother* house with the House of Reps and turkey slaps Bronwyn Bishop.

The Internet, Eh?

These days the lines between journalist and punter have blurred. Journos used to sneer at the internet until the circulation figures of the newspapers they work for came in one day and the penny dropped. Now all journalists have at least three blogs and are forever tinkering around in HTML and other things they're too drunk to understand.

The good old days of the Guild of Drunken Journalists as the gatekeepers of all knowledge are over. They've been replaced by bloggers with a stethoscope on the pulse and the world's breaking news at their fingertips.

Sadly, most bloggers waste the opportunity, preferring to ramble on and on about the tedious details of their meaningless lives, their pets, their disgusting skin diseases and associated trivia of no interest to anyone including themselves.

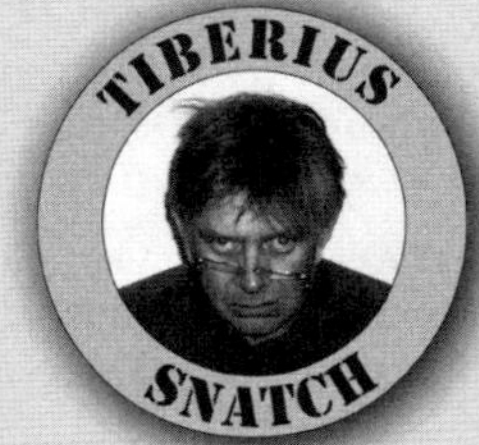

The Myth of the Internet

The internet does not exist. The whole thing's a hoax. Have you ever *seen* it? Have you ever *licked* it?

It's disturbing because every time the government wants to give Rupert Murdoch more of what he wants, they justify it by saying the internet has changed the media landscape. This is a nonsense. It's like saying that Darrell Lea should be given a monopoly on confectionery because of the technological changes the Easter Bunny has wrought on the chocolate delivery industry.

I once pulled up a so-called IT specialist as she was scurrying along the corridors of *The Sydney Morning Herald* (what do these people do for a living anyway?) and I asked her where the internet actually, physically exists. Her answer was that it was a bunch of zeroes and ones living inside a bunch of hard drives somewhere. Or it might have been number ones and number twos. I forget. The whole thing sounds about as plausible as Scientology to me.

You may protest that you have 'seen' the internet on a screen. Well every night I 'see' Kerry O'Brien on my TV screen, but as any TV insider will tell you, Kerry doesn't exist either; he's merely a strange trick of the light that occurs when you refract a light beam through a glass jug filled with suet and horsehair.

Prove I lie.

Jack's Final Thoughts on the Media in Australia

In a matter of months Steve Irwin, Kerry Packer, Peter Brock and colourful Sydney businessman Abe Saffron all passed away. Jack the Insider was moved to pen this eulogy of Abe, which ran for eighty-three pages in the Dapto Dogs Form Guide. *An excerpt is printed below.*

My Friends,

In recent times, we have had to endure the passing of a handful of Australians who none of us have met and indeed would not care to meet ante-mortem. But oh, how we have wept. Wept until our tear ducts shat themselves and collapsed. And then we wept some more.

You see, Australians are a bunch of necrophiliacs – hotfooting it after funeral corteges, blubbing as we go, prying off coffin lids with a Phillips head screwdriver and locking ourselves in urgent, fumbling embrace with the dead.

Peter Brock – 'Brockie' – had five memorial services. That's three more than Pope John Paul II, two more than Mother Teresa and four more than Mahatma Gandhi, whose lifeless corpse was dispatched with a Bic lighter and four litres of distillate after he was blasted off his perch in 1948. I reckon it may have been more appropriate to take Brockie's arms and legs off and dump his body down the Merri Creek in one of Melbourne's more troubled northern suburbs – a popular burial ground for clapped-out automotive bits and pieces – but I suppose it would have been un-Australian.

The Stingray Guy, Steve Irwin, was feted in death for a month on our television screens and in the print media. Let's face it, when he was alive, I wouldn't have pissed on him if he was self-immolating. Now, his death mask is up for auction on eBay and at last glance was fetching a cool three hundred million dollars.

The only exception to the Australian rule for 'dead-uns' appears to be Abe Saffron. Now old Abe made a quid out of giving a man a beer and a root on a Sunday, and we can all agree that this was a noble pursuit. He was an affirmative action employer, too, long before it became de rigueur in the rest of the community. And like Brockie and Irwin, Saffron departed this mortal coil doing something he loved – giving a hot shot to a prostitute.

Steve Irwin: even in death a shameless attention seeker

Yet when Abe passed over to the other side, there was a rush to demonise him that I can only describe as unseemly. Dead men can't sue of course and so journalists simply ignored the facts, reached for the thesaurus, looked under 'S' and pronounced the old man a 'scumbag'.

But Abe Saffron notwithstanding, I put it to you now that all you've got to be is dead in this country and no-one will say a bad word about you.

When he was still around, Kerry Packer had a rather nasty habit of crushing the life out of stupid businessmen and unfortunate sex workers. Sadly, both were in the wrong place at the wrong time.

He was the dumbest punter I've ever seen and I've spent a day at the track with Hawkie. If Big Kezza tipped you into a horse it would invariably run sideways down the straight and come home stone motherless last. Smart punters knew to give him a big swerve.

But on Boxing Day last year, Big Kezza's rancid vital organs finally gave out and he was off.

Now, I don't know if Big Kezza is now a slap-up meal for assorted lichen and fungi. Maybe he's strumming gently on a harp astride one of your weightier clouds. Or spit roasting over a slow flame with Satan poking him in the guts with a stick, asking, 'You still think there's nothin' fuckin' here, pal?'

But what I do know is in life the man was a shit. Indeed Kerry Packer assumed the sobriquet like a badge of honour. But when he became a dead shit, the entire nation donned the black gear and flicked onto Channel Nine, sobbing without restraint. We'd still be watching today if some of the fools at Channel Nine could figure out how to turn Kezza's funeral into a 104-part reality show.

And we feasted on anecdotes of the Big Fella's alleged sense of charity which, in truth, amounted to little more than him not pointing and laughing at the homeless on the odd occasion.

As Australians, we can do nothing else but eulogise the dead with maudlin hyperbole. Maybe it's guilt, I don't know. I often think about old Kerry. Could I have done more for him? Maybe I should have watched 'Our Place' with that tiresome chippy Scott Cam and his sidekick Cherie Hausler before it got the arse after three episodes. Or maybe if I hadn't flicked through the channels during a break in the cricket. It troubles me to this day. If I could have done more, it may have spared us all from Eddie McGuire, who tragically remains respiring to this day.

Apparently, dead is the place to be in this country. Now, I hope – indeed I pray – for the day that I will be strapped to the back of a guncarriage, while the nation looks on, sobbing helplessly. But it's not going to happen anytime soon, or at least not until my next car accident. And that's the problem. We're not dying nearly quickly enough – despite the best efforts of the Victorian Police Force. So the dead remain in the absolute minority, and the moment rigor mortis sets in, those of us who remain earthbound lose our minds.

CHAPTER SIX

Culture

'Whenever I hear the word culture, I reach for my revolver'

Hermann Göring

Culture in Australia

From the outside Australian culture seems like a complex and forbidding place. The reality is once you front up to the counter, buy a ticket and go inside, you realise the whole thing is pretty simple, because everyone thinks the same way. People in 'The Arts' like to use words like 'edgy', 'radical' and 'contentious', but if anyone pipes up with some second thoughts about second-wave feminism, they're belted over the head and escorted from the building. The whole thing can be covered pretty quickly.

This is all you need to know.

Australia's Writers

Writers are people who lie for a living. And yet, when these bastards are caught red-handed perpetrating identity fraud, everyone falls about in surprise. Helen Demidenko turned out to be as Ukrainian as a Sao biscuit. Norma Khouri said she was being oppressed by Muslims in Jordan, when it turns out the whole time she'd been having a month-long hair appointment elsewhere. Wanda Koolmatrie and Ern Malley were figments of the diseased imagination of some dickhead with a hard-on for the Australia Council.

What you and most people don't know is that the scandal runs deeper. Much deeper.

Patrick White

The grand old poof of Australian letters was nothing of the sort. I can reveal here that all his works were secretly written by Ernie Sigley. Did you ever see both men together at the same time? Well, did you?

Miles Franklin

Inspiration to feminists everywhere, the author of *My Brilliant Career* was in fact the former giant of Rugby League, Rex Mossop.

Peter Carey

There is no such person as Peter Carey. I know this for a fact because I am deeply implicated in the production of his work. I keep a large basement in my house where several thousand chimps flail away at typewriters all day in exchange for a handful of bananas and a scratch on the backside. Every two years one of these gifted chimps happens to type out something vaguely coherent and I ship it off to the publisher on a don't-ask-don't-tell basis.

Les Murray

Les isn't a human being either. Les is in fact an empty Humpty Dumpty costume from a children's party that was held in 1957.

BIN NIGHT

A poem by Tiberius Snatch which takes the form of a sonnet in a deliberately unspecified number of lines, almost constructed in iambic pentameter – a form of verse invented by the poet and therefore rightly called a 'Snatch Sonnet', a fact about which he will not be gainsaid.

'Tis one decade and more since Camelot
Became a house divided by itself
And yea is now just talked about a lot
Brought down by the Poisonous Elf, himself

In tears, three tiers, our government descends,
And pall he in the dunnest smoke of hell
Who sends the men of lowest form to tend
To those of us who live with sewage smells

Suburbia is not for faint of heart –
It cometh as the rate the payer forks
To those who counsel in the form of counc-il
For right to dwell where once *indigenes* stalked looking for oysters

Does local council see not those bereft
When all that is not Otto-binned is left?

Bin night! And not a creature is stirring
Not even a mouse – in the Lower House
Where I sit and gaze forlornly at the string
That held the photo of Paul Keating's house

Bin night! Nor feet nor metre can contain the ire
That burneth in my true believer's heart
For citizens who lost the Muse of fire
And voted in a righteous little fart

Bin night! The souls of Chif and Curtin rue an age!
And into my back passage slowly creep
As garbologists outside my front passage
Empty bins and in my windows peep

Right-wing heathen sympathisers all –
I've seen them drinking *lattes* in the mall

Bin night! 'What light from yonder window breaks?
'Tis *The Sun,* nay, *The Age* he reads,' they shriek
Then to their mayor all, they softly make
To tell of what they saw when in they peeked

Bin night! And polystyrene cannot hold my bile
It falleth like the acid rain from heaven
Upon the place beneath. It is twice vile –
I pray it poisons John and blesseth Kevin

Bin night! Oh Hawke! Oh squawk! Oh ruptured spleen!
Who breathed most foul of Liberal-scented air
I see conspiracy and where it's been
And what they did to Cheryl wasn't fair

Bin night! Bin Laden! Bit pissed! Beg pardon!

Bin night! 'Bin night's no time to vent your spleen!'
My neighbours all, they come out for to shout
'Tomorrow you can tell it to The Greens –
Tonight shut up! And ... *put your rubbish out!*

'And furthermore, you pontificating prat, your pathetic
political drivel
Gives us all the shits!
You can't even make it scan or rhyme
Except some of the time
In little bits!'

The Art World

Everytime I hear the word 'Art' my eyes glaze over and I know I'm about to be exposed to something knocked out by a smack addict that's supposed to be good for me.

I used to find artists were great to get on the drink with. They were generally quick with a shout and didn't have a clue what to do with money, so when they came into a bit of cash, I found standing within close proximity to them to be a very profitable place to be.

Nowadays, artists don't want to be artists, they want to be celebrities. Sure they'll tell you they wear their personal integrity like a badge of honour. But when someone offers them a truckload of cash, they'll hurl themselves off the Harbour Bridge with a sparkler stuck up their dates while singing 'Nearer My God to Me'. All in the name of art. The art world is no stranger to 'controversy'. When Andres Serrano brought his 'important' work *Piss Christ* to Australia there was a huge reaction from the churches, who were upset that someone had dunked a crucifix in a great big glass of his own urine and called it 'Art' for christ's sake. I was upset too, because I knew that Serrano had been on the gear and his urine was likely to be so cloudy the kiddies mightn't get a good look at Jesus on the cross. I rang him and offered him three gallons of my own premium piss instead but he was having none of it. I wrote him off as a temperamental wanker and swore off having anything to do with contemporary art again.

That was until I got the call from Jeff Koons. Koonsy had achieved some notoriety by posting some stills of his home videos with Italian porn star Cicciolina in a gallery. So the obvious next step in his career was to pop over to Sydney's Museum of Contemporary Art and create a giant puppy made of flowers to sit in front of the MCA on Circular Quay.

I used to tend to the puppy, but it became a pain in the arse, so I just let it go. Pretty soon, the pup had flowers growing out of his coit and up through his nostrils. He looked so bad I thought it was only a matter of time before the RSPCA turned up to put him out of his misery. I guess that must have been what happened because one day I turned up with a cherry picker to pick the weeds out of his gonads and the bugger had gone.

Still it was a top bit of art and had it all over anything that has ever been done in Australia.

I know what you're thinking. What about Australia's great painters? What about Tom Roberts, Sidney Nolan, William Dobell, Arthur Streeton, Albert Tucker and Brett Whiteley? I know these blokes were handy with a texta, dab hands with a Derwent and living gods with a crayon in hand but when it comes to knocking up a gigantic topiary dog, they wouldn't know where to start.

WRAPPED IN PLASTIC

Few people are aware that Surfers Paradise is not actually a city, but an art installation assembled by the great Bulgarian artist Christo. He delivered it to the Queensland Government on the back of a truck, back in 1969, wrapped in vast amounts of plastic sheeting. Joh loved it and encouraged people to move in. The silly old bugger never realised Christo was taking the piss, and that he wasn't supposed to take the sheeting off.

How To Speak Just Like Art Guys

Art galleries are great places to get a feed and score pseudoephedrine. But you need to speak the lingo to get in. Cut this out, stick it on the back of your hand and help yourself to as much free vino and finger food as you like.

- **Playful:** Any work of art with a TV reference. For instance: you spot a bloodstained sanitary pad glued on top of a black-and-white telly playing a video of *Gilligan's Island*, well you can safely call that 'playful'.
- **Discourse:** Fancy name for talking and that. About art.
- **Kitsch:** If it's on a gallery wall, it's good. If it's in a McMansion? Bad.
- **Hilarious:** When you're supposed to be laughing with the artist.
- **Appropriation:** A florid term for a serious breach of copyright. Artists are forever pinching images and ideas from one another. The term 'appropriation' sounds so much nicer than 'theft'.
- **Gendered:** Something created by a girl who makes her own clothes.
- **Deconstruction:** Pulling something apart to find underlying, hidden meanings, as in: 'Sandra spent six months deconstructing the patriarchical subtext of Bunnings catalogues to prepare her next installation titled *Fuck U Daddy Reticulated Sprinkler System*.
- **Vigorous:** Drugfucked.
- **Emotive:** See above.
- **Polemical:** A rant from a state-subsidised artist complaining about how unfair it all is. Normally something dunked in the artist's urine, which is a bit of a cack, eh?
- **Dialogue:** a conversation between inanimate objects, as in: 'Simon cleverly places the cinder block in dialogue with the wallpaper in this installation.'

I Don't Know Much About Art But I Do Like Adolf Hitler's

You can accrue all the power and money you like (and you will after you've read this book) but it all counts for naught if you're casually dismissed as a Bulgarian.

When it comes to art, the first thing you need to do is have the guts to back your instincts. Don't just hang the stuff on the walls with a couple of screws and a length of wire. Araldite your art to the walls. It's your way of saying, 'I like this gear so much, it's never coming down.'

If you're short of a quid my advice to you is to make your own art. Back in the late eighties I had a ketamine toasted sandwich and forgot who I was for a while. I woke up three days later with every stick of furniture in splinters and the crockery stomped into a fine powder. The hotel hit me with a bill for $200,000. Then I had a moment of pure inspiration. I pronounced the room a work in progress by contemporary artist, Julian Schnabel. Then I emptied a forty-four-gallon drum of sump oil on the floor and sold the room to the drummer from Metallica and managed to come out of it twenty large to the good.

That's the sort of quick thinking you need to make a quid in the art world. Quality doesn't count for anything so be resourceful. Have a look around the house and see what you can find. It paid off for me.

I had a rummage around in the garage at home a while back and I came across some old watercolours painted by Adolf Hitler. What with the war an' all, I'd completely forgotten I had them.

There are twenty-one of them and very nice they are too. Adolf Hitler may have been a vicious genocidal maniac but he had a great sense of perspective and clearly knew his way around an easel.

Hitler's watercolours make sense to me. The man knew how to paint a tree. You can look at his paintings and say, there's a road, there's a shed, there's a river and the sky is blue.

The one criticism I do have is there are no people in any of the 'Dolftser's paintings. I think it's a sign of his personal angst and deep, abiding ennui, quite frankly.

Adolf Hitler could paint a tree and the sky was always blue

Just looking at his paintings it's obvious that he didn't like people much, so it's no great surprise that when he came to power in 1933 he had a lot of them killed.

But when you compare Adolf Hitler's works to that of his artistic contemporaries, he comes up trumps. Modernists, dadaists, cubists: incomprehensible and pointless, the lot of them. Picasso could only paint sheilas with three noses and four eyes. And Salvador Dali – I dunno what he was drinking at the time he knocked up some of that surrealist rubbish but whatever it was, I'd like a couple of schooners right now.

The dadaist Marcel Duchamp pencilled in a moustache and beard on the *Mona Lisa* and had the temerity to call it art. But without the good wholesome stuff knocked up by people like Adolf Hitler, Duchamp would not have had a pot to piss in.

And who can say what might have happened to the world if Adolf hadn't got knocked back by the Academy of Fine Arts in Vienna back in 1912. The academy may have been a little hasty in rejecting him. I'm sure if they had their time over again, they might change their minds and send him a very nice personal invitation to come and refine his obvious talents.

But before you knew it, Adolf had left Vienna, feeling angry and disillusioned, and dashed off to fight in World War I. He seemed to find his niche there and couldn't wait to kick off the sequel. It's always the way. You put a man in uniform and he turns into Adolf Hitler.

But if the Viennese Art Academy had given him a gig, I think we can safely say there'd be a lot more artists about today.

Australian Cinema

A few decades ago the Australian film industry was a fun place to be. All you had to do was take a couple of polaroids of Hanging Rock with a few sheilas running up the side of it. Chuck some panpipe music over the top of it and you had a hit on your hands. In those days the government kept the whole industry afloat by allowing a generous tax write-off on film investment that became known as 10BA.

It was the best rort I've ever invented and it kept me in schooners and swan for the best part of a decade. Fred Schepisi, Bruce Beresford and Richard Franklin used to swear by it and we'd often pop down to Canberra to get on the piss, apply for a grant and put our hands up for a serious tax deduction.

But when Phillip Adams got rich, the penny dropped for the government and the 10BA rort got scaled back. The Fraser Government was fearful of the urban blight of derelict filmmakers trawling the streets, hitting up punters for the price of a schooner and a packet of Viscount Slims, so they replaced the rort with government subsidies. This allowed Australian filmmakers to make 'personal statements', as opposed to profit and loss statements and before you could say 'Bert Newton in *Fatty Finn*', the whole industry went down the brasco.

Jack on Cinema: Ingmar Bergman and Me

When the great Ingmar Bergman died in July 2007, Jack the Insider was invited to pen this obituary for Greyhounds and Gravlax Weekly, *the bible for enthusiasts of racing and Scandinavian cinema.*

I'm a big fan of your classic Aussie feel-good flick. But like most Australians, I'm also partial to bleak, atmospheric Swedish cinema. I've been close to many of the giants of Swedish filmmaking, particularly the late Ingmar Bergman. Tragically, too many Australians remain ignorant of Ingmar's full contribution to our cultural life.

No man had a bigger influence on the Australian thoroughbred racing industry. The great Swedish director takes up more space than an IKEA warehouse in the imagination of we horsey folk.

We will never forget his achievements in 1984, winning four Academy Awards for his autobiographical pic 'Fanny and Alexander' and then going on to salute at the leger to win the Wakeful, Moir and Turnbull Stakes. That he did so while attired as a feudal Scandinavian monarch is further to his credit and helped draw the crowds back to the stands.

By his own admission, Ingmar Bergman was not the fastest jockey in this country. He would often get a ride in the bush and while the rest of the field galloped the 1600 metres in a slick one minute, thirty-five seconds, Ingmar would get his nag out of the barriers, pull it to the rails and get it around the six furlongs in a tick under six hours, using a riding method known to fans of the equine arts as Brechtian alienation technique.

Despite his legion of adoring fans in the racing industry, no-one's ever gotten to the bottom of his films. Until now, that is. I can reveal that Ingmar told me everything just before he died in July 2007.

Ingmar had been crook for a while and I'd heard he didn't have long left. We'd chatted a couple of years back; I tried to get him a ride on Maybe Mahal and tip him in to a nice little romantic comedy, starring Steve Martin, J. Lo and The Rock. But Ingmar seemed unable to give it his full attention. The poor bloke was stuck in anomie and just couldn't get out of it.

He rang me a couple of weeks back and he told me this time he was really on the way out. So I took it upon myself to get over to the remote Swedish island of Fårö as quickly as I could.

Most people in the film caper hold old Ingmar up as a technical genius but the truth is that no-one has a clue what he was on about. That's why Ingmar Bergman, the man I think of as Sweden's Roy Higgins, spewed his guts up to me for four days on end before he sat up, farted and left this mortal coil.

He reeled off his films in perfect chronological order and told me what he was trying to achieve in each and every one of them – for example, his 1973 film, 'Scenes from a Marriage', the grim footage of the slow, painful destruction of a relationship. At an economical 320 minutes it's a joy to watch over and over, but it turns out Ingmar didn't mean to make the film that long. He told me he'd walked off the set and got on the turps for a couple of hours, leaving the camera running. Forgot the thing was on. When he got back, he just packed up and took off. He ran the film holus-bolus at advance screenings, without so much as a cursory edit. No-one seemed to notice or mind, so he just let it go.

With tears rolling down his cheeks, Ingmar told me of his pain in not rendering 'Seventh Seal – The Musical' into celluloid. He spoke of his frustration at never having worked with Stallone, Willis or Sandler, referring to them as 'the Masters'. He even had a good word for Hoges.

Ingmar told me he was the one who encouraged Stallone to take a gamble; to put the shooters down and do a bit of comedy. It surprised me to learn that he was the driving force behind the production of the 1992 film, 'Stop or My Mom Will Shoot'. He even played a cameo in the film, appearing as Estelle Getty's gynaecologist.

The iconoclastic filmmaker bared his soul to me for the best part of a week. We'd sleep through the morning and then in the afternoon we'd sit back and watch the races on the telly for a while. One bleak afternoon Ingmar was getting knocked around on the punt so he got to his feet and challenged me to a game of chess. It's a matter of record that I gave him a thorough hiding. His predictable use of the Queen's Gambit Declined and the Sicilian Defence exposed his knights and after that it was just a matter of time before I put his king to the sword.

The poor old sod kept pleading for a double or nothing rematch but I wasn't having any of that. I'd already flogged him at Scrabble and I couldn't see any point in humiliating him further. He took off in a huff, saying he was going to have a long lie-down.

When he didn't turn up for a breakfast beer, I knew something was amiss. He'd moved on. Passed away. Just like that.

In a way it was a big relief when he finally turned his toes up. At least now, I'd never have to sit through another turgid black-and-white movie set in medieval Sweden.

I love a good funeral and Ingmar Bergman's was no exception. The aquavit flowed all day and well into the night. Max von Sydow and I had a bit of a good natured wrestle on the beach. Liv Ullmann put the hard word on me at one point but I put that down to the drink. Sting turned up and played the lute.

I was glad I got along to see off Ingmar Bergman. He was a top bloke; a deadset monument to dark, incomprehensible cinema and a man who, for mine, was desperately unlucky not to win the 1973 Victorian jockey's premiership.

We will not see his like again.

Ingmar Bergman: gone to the great racecourse in the sky

The Music Scene

Paul McCartney rips into an enormous skull bong erected in his honour by the people of Melbourne in 1964

Live music used to be a good caper in Australia. In Melbourne back in the seventies I was a bit of a sharpie: I used to put on my black and red Connie jacket of a Saturday night and drive out in the Monaro to a beer barn out in Essendon to see Lobby Loyde and the Coloured Balls. The place was packed with high-spirited working-class lads like me leaping about having a tremendous time of it. That was suburban culture in those days. And what do the kids have today: a bunch of hippies with credit cards like Missy Higgins and the John Butler Trio, who exhort us to turn off a few light bulbs and drag the Malvern Stars out of the garage? In the old days, a good chunk of black tar heroin would have seen these bastards off but nowadays these so-called rock stars are alarmingly fit and don't do drugs. They're a fucking disgrace to the business.

I blame the Beatles actually. They were a top outfit in 1964 when they toured here. Paul McCartney was a fresh-faced young bloke with a powerful thirst for the piss and the drugs. Now he's a vegan in a cardigan. I mean, what sort of example is he setting for young Aussie kiddies, keen to plug into a Marshall amp and make a bit of noise?

Any self-respecting kiddie would take a look at McCartney as he is now, give the music industry the flick and turn to a career in Australian Rules football. The money's better, drugs are all over the place and you don't have to pretend you like Molly Meldrum. No wonder the music scene's in the shithouse.

Theatre in Australia

I'm strongly of the view that theatre is a place you go to only when you've got a sheila to impress. I'm beyond all that now so I can't see myself going there ever again.

CHAPTER SEVEN

Money

It is easier to pass wind through the eye of a camel than it is for a poor man to enter the Melbourne Club

Luke 4:3 (but don't quote me on that)

Economics in Australia

Adam Smith: a man who, essentially, did nothing for Australia

Economics was invented by a bloke called Adam Smith. He was Scottish, which means he wasn't Australian. As far as I know, he didn't even have a credit card.

Smithy claimed to have discovered the 'invisible hand' of the market; he found it in his PJs one cold Tuesday morning in Edinburgh and felt invigorated enough to put pen to paper.

Over the next ten days, with the aid of several schooners of Drambuie and a plate of raw haggis, Smithy knocked out his classic work, *The Wealth of Nations*, which went on to become the most popular unread book in the world until Stephen Hawking's *A Brief History of Time*.

Smithy's point was this: so long as every individual remains hell-bent on ruthlessly pursuing their own interests, then the greater good for the whole of society will somehow be accomplished as well. In recent years Rwanda, Somalia and the former Yugoslavia have given this idea its fullest expression, yet amazingly, many of these places are still to get their own Starbucks.

Smithy's whole philosophy can be boiled down to this famous sentence:

> *It is not from the benevolence of the butcher, the brewer, or the baker that we expect our dinner, but from their regard to their own interest.*

That's all very well, but what if I need a couple of chops and some garlic bread at half past seven on a Friday night and those lazy shits are pursuing their own interests by going home to watch *Big Brother*, Smithy? What about my needs, you tedious Scottish prick?

WILSON TUCKEY'S FANTABULOUS CONTRAPTION

It's one of life's great ironies that the world's oil supplies are only found in its most dangerous parts. If there's a skull and crossbones on the map, there's bound to be plenty of oil underground thereabouts. It's God's joke on all of us and he's whooping it up in heaven as we speak.

The economy is up shit creek unless we can rid ourselves of our oil dependency. People keep talking about alternatives – alcohol and whatnot, but this seems to me to be an utter waste of a perfectly good drink. And what would we tell Mel Gibson if he pops down here for a holiday? We're all out of tequila but he can go to the servo and pump a couple of litres of ethanol straight into his alimentary canal? That would be un-Australian.

I have been a strong advocate for the trade of uranium to the Iranians for their juice. We've got uranium just lying around on the ground around here. Meanwhile, the Iranians are having to make do with second-rate uranium from the Congo. Now our government won't have a bar of it but I think a straight swap of a jumbo full of Australian uranium for a couple of hundred megalitres of Tehran tea could solve this country's energy problems overnight. Or it could set back human civilisation for fifty thousand years or so, but, regardless of the possible outcomes, I think we have to pursue what's in the national interest.

But back to our energy crisis. The good news is that our pollies are doing their bit. And that brings me to my old mate Wilson Tuckey: Australia's oldest parliamentarian and a great patriot who reckons he's got the whole thing fixed.

It all started when we were throwing back a few schooners of liquid hydrogen and Old Ironbar let rip with a bottom burp that knocked us both over and shot a jet of blue flame two metres long out of his trousers.

Wilson's not a smart man but I could tell from the look in his eyes that he'd had a brief moment of clarity and ever since then we've been hunkered down in his garage working on a hydrogen car prototype.

And I'm happy to tell you that we've done it. V8 GT 351, twin carbies, chevvy brakes, chevvy shocks, a very nice paint job. It looks like a winner to me. The only problem we have is backing the car up to Wilson's backside so he can fill it up. Our long national nightmare of petroleum dependence will be over just as soon as Wilson can locate a funnel.

Will somebody get Wilson Tuckey a funnel, already?

Free Trade Versus Protection

By 1901 Australia had federated. The leaders Barton, Deakin and Reid joined together for a couple of choruses of 'Kum Ba Yah' in celebration, then it was back to bitter, undying hatred and enmity.

The Tariff Wall: it kept us safe from hordes of low-price Chinese toys for decades

The issue that split them was an economic one: should we let in a flood of imports and make the locals compete? Or should we stick up a tariff wall, along with a dingo fence and a big sign at Bondi that says, 'No Poofs or Asians'?

Alfie Deakin won that one for the protectionists. The tariff wall went up and stayed up until 1983 when Paul Keating went out to buy a locally made jumper and realised that he could buy a Mitsubishi Pajero for the same price.

The wall was dismantled and Australia was swamped by cheap underpants and VCRs. It was a nightmare.

The Nightmare of Competition

Australian manufacturers now had to make goods that people wanted and, on top of that, they had to work as well. It was a double blow from which they never recovered.

Victoria and South Australia, the manufacturing heartlands, were gutted.

Melbourne, a town populated by more sanctimonious, humourless leftists than any other city in the world, has had a crack at a comedy festival. Adelaide is still struggling to get a Cold Chisel cover band–led recovery off the ground, but the premier doesn't really have his heart in it.

Calm Down, Everything's Fine

But it's all been for the best. Australia is enjoying its longest burst of uninterrupted economic growth in its history. And wouldn't you just know it, it's all thanks to China. They sell us their plasma screen TVs and running shoes, and in return we sell them vast chunks of our raw minerals while we educate their kiddies. There's a ton of it still left, so you've got nothing to worry about.

The Budget

The Budget Lockup: Worse Than Abu Ghraib

Every year, sometime in May, a disgraceful cruelty is perpetrated on a small group of people in Canberra.

A bunch of thirsty journalists are locked in a room which has no alcohol, television or pornography. They're handed a massive document filled with jargon, lies and complex diagrams, and they're told they have to make sense of it within three hours. The whole thing is simply inhumane and probably in violation of the Geneva Convention.

This is called the Budget Lockup. Much is expected of these journos, but all they're able to do in that time is to gorge themselves on tea and Milk Arrowroots while they try to tease out the nuances of the fat printout in front of them.

A journalist on Budget Day: cruel and unusual punishment. If it happened to anyone other than journalists, there'd be howls of outrage.

No wonder they tend to miss the crucial disclaimers buried on page 5722 of the document, such as 'Cheques will not be honoured' and 'Help, I'm stuck in the basement at Treasury and I need my medication.'

All facts and figures in that Budget document sound plausible, but in fact they are completely worthless. Typically, there'll be a table like this:

	2007–08
GST revenue*	$40,067,945.05

See that little *? That leads to a tiny footnote that says '*(proj.)'. This is short for 'projected', or 'Don't hold me to this figure, I'm hoping I'll have a job at Macquarie Bank when all of this falls through.'

Most journalists have got no hope of decoding all that. By definition, all journos must be economically illiterate. It stands to reason. Otherwise they'd have pissed off to the financial sector ages ago and would be on their third wife and second Ferrari by now.

Budget Night

Then at 7.30 pm the treasurer gets to his feet in the House of Representatives and tells us who gets what. He says it's your money, but deep down, in his heart of hearts, he really thinks it's his.

The treasurer burbles away excitedly, while 149 narcissists are compelled to sit still and listen in agonised silence for a whole thirty minutes. The prime minister has little to do in that half-hour except study the treasurer's backside through the folds of his gabardine slacks. After twenty-five minutes he knows the contours of that bum better than the back of his own hand.

Meanwhile back in the lockup, the journos have given up trying to master the details. They call their editors and last year's Budget headline is pasted in once again for tomorrow's lift-out guide: 'BEER, CIGS UP'.

Bracket Creeps

The sad thing is that it's all completely unnecessary. Back when Chif was treasurer, the Budget was done on the back of an envelope at his kitchen table in Bathurst. When he ran out of fingers and toes, he'd ask his missus to take off her shoes. It worked a treat.

Frank Crean was treasurer in the Whitlam Government and he tried the same thing but he lost his envelope and so his government was rightly denounced as a pack of economic illiterates. The envelope was later found in the 'Misc' section of Mrs Crean's spice rack but by then it was too late.

The big reforms came through when Paul Keating got the job. He floated the dollar back in 1984 and since then it's been jerking back and forth like a rottweiler on a bungee cord. He got into trouble when the economy hit the skids. He was reported to have said the famous words, 'This is the recession that Australia had to have.' But he never said it. I was there at that media conference and I distinctly heard Paul say, 'This is the procession, hat, ostriches, battered sav.' Even I'm not sure what he meant by that.

Anyway, despite his best efforts as treasurer, Paul found himself presiding over record interest rates and catastrophic unemployment. The Labor Party thought long and hard and decided there was only one place he could go: the prime ministership.

The Libs took over and my old mate Petey Costello got the job. Petey brought down twelve budgets and got sick to death of it. Every year you could see the tops of his ears fold down even lower.

Petey's done his best; he's tried to be as much like Keating as possible. Paul dismissed him as 'all tip and no iceberg', which I thought was grossly unfair. There's plenty of iceberg down there.

Peter Costello rightly tells Mr Speaker to shove it up his arse as he delivers the 2003 budget. Or is it 2006? No, wait, isn't that 1997?

Economic Jargon Explained

The Current Account Deficit, yesterday

Whenever pinheads want to convince you that what they're up to is beyond the realms of normal human understanding, they'll sit down and create a bunch of meaningless phrases and terms designed to shroud a subject in darkness.

Keating thought he'd brought us all up to speed. The truth is we all just nodded politely while he babbled on about 'J curves' and 'First Order Stochatic Dominance'. Then, after he left, we checked our wallets and discovered that we still had enough left for a schooner and a packet of fags. So the economy was going okay, eh?

My mate J.K. Galbraith was completely shameless about making economics a deep, abiding riddle to the masses. He wrote a ton of books in the full knowledge that he was the only one who would ever understand them. He didn't give a bugger that no-one bought his books. He didn't need the cash. J.K. was an economist and therefore pretty canny with a quid. If he was ever struggling for a shout, he'd blame it all on the Frederickson Quotient or the Benn Indicator.

I always knew he was taking the piss but US governments from Roosevelt to Johnson didn't have a clue what he was on about. Fearing a terrible depression, they handed him more money to go and invent some more economic mumbo jumbo to keep the populace happy and forking out for a new fridge or telly every couple of years. He was a class act, J.K. A tremendous bloke to get on the turps with and, what's more, he really knew his way around a brothel.

AUSTRALIAN FISCAL POLICY: A REAPPRAISAL

If you ask me the worst thing that mongrel Howard ever did was to bring in a GST. It's regressive, it's inequitable and it does nothing to accommodate our greatest national characteristic: our love of gambling.

When I was placed thirteenth on Pauline's One Nation senate ticket in 1998, I gave her an alternative policy.

My idea was simple: establish the GST on a scratchie-based system. You scratch away on the back of the price tag to figure out how much GST you pay on any given item.

That way most of us would pay bugger-all. A few would have to pay a few bucks here and there. And some unlucky bastard would get hit with a thousand bucks GST on a Mars Bar. Shit, it would have worked beautifully.

Pauline said she'd think about it and I was over the moon. But then she went off to shout at a bunch of blacks who were standing too close to her car and she forgot all about it.

But it came very close to becoming official One Nation policy. And given that Howard coopted most of her other policies, it shows you how close it was to getting up. That's an exciting thought, isn't it but?

Econo-babble	What It Really Means
Arbitrage	Buying low, selling high.
Balance of Payments	How much we owe the Chinese at any given time.
Balanced Budget	The government has stopped spending on trivial matters such as education, health and roads.
Capitation	Much less troubling than decapitation.
Consumer Confidence	Never mind that we're in a depression, you've still got your credit card, right?
Consumer Price Index	The price of bananas, raffia lamps and gusseted pantihose tossed together to determine if we've hit hyper-inflation yet.
Deflation	When prices go down. This almost never happens.
Demand	When you've got a powerful thirst.
Depression	Something to really spoil your day, but don't worry, the next world war should see it off.
Deregulation	Letting business off the leash so they can get on with the important business of kicking off the next global depression.
Fiat Money	Money that is intrinsically useless, so why not buy a crap Italian car?
Hyperbolic Discounting	A practice used by disreputable mobile phone dealers whose prices are so low that fears are held for their sanity.
Intensive Margin	You worked how many hours at $8.25 an hour?
Labour Economics	Sign the AWA already or your arse is out the door.
Recession	Time to sell the house and move into that caravan you've always wanted.
Structural Adjustment Programs	A clever way to squeeze even more money out of the Third World.
Supply	How quickly the breweries can make it.

GREAT! DEPRESSION!

It's a sad fact that many decent Australians were reduced to cannibalism during the Great Depression. My dear old nanna confessed she had little choice but to chain up homeless labourers in her basement and feast upon them one by one as the need arose. Nanna was even forced to knit a suit of human flesh just to keep warm through the winter. It was unseemly, but it must have done the old girl the world of good: even in her nineties, my Nan still runs a sprightly market stall. Her apricot jam's okay, but you'd be wise to give the pâté a miss.

J.K. GALBRAITH HAGGLES WITH HOOKERS

THEN OUR HERO GOES A STEP TOO FAR...
YOU KNOW, I COULD CONVINCE THE PRESIDENT TO NATIONALISE THE LOT OF YOU.
CYRUS! CYRUS! THIS HERE WHITE BOY DON'T CARE FOR YOUR ASSET PRICING MODEL!
OH HE DON'T, DO HE?
GOD DAMNED NEO-KEYNESIAN ECONOMISTS!
THEY TALK THE TALK, BUT WHEN IT COME TO PERSONAL FISCAL POLICY...
... AIN'T NUTHIN' BUT A BUNCH O' FRIEDMANITE-MONETARIST ASSHOLES...
... WHY DON'CHOO LET ME REDISTRIBUTE THIS PIPE O' YOURS, WHITEBOY...
AND SO...
I REALLY MISS THE BARTER ECONOMY...!
END.

Merchant Banking: Why It's Not Just Rhyming Slang

Macquarie Bank chief executive Allan Moss is a good mate of mine; good for a laugh and a day at the races. And the man knows how to lunch. We start with a few aperitifs at dawn on Monday morning, then we dine on swan and panda, all washed down with a few schooners of Château Lafite. We normally finish up about three o'clock in the morning, belting around the streets in a Lamborghini taunting the homeless.

There's a lot of talk in the lefty media that the chief executive of Macquarie Bank is a tick or two overpaid. But the truth is Allan Moss is barely scraping by. And I know he's very unhappy that Macquarie Bank thought it fit to fling him only thirty-three million this year.

Last time we lunched he was weeping and crying poor. I had to pick up the tab and let me tell you roasted leg of panda in a red wine reduction is not a cheap feed. All I could tell poor Allan is that he needs to work a bit harder; get his head down and knock out a few private equity deals and top his salary up to a far more reasonable one million a week.

Buy Qantas at a bargain basement price, I said, and strip and sell the lot. Flog energy company Alinta to the Mafia. Do some good work for Macquarie Bank, I told him, and they'd reward him in turn.

He told me he's not sure how he's going to make ends meet. He's a victim, in my view: a victim of the spiralling cost of living in this country.

Yesterday during lunch he put the hard word on me for a loan. I was going to knock him back but after he offered a few international airports, the Pacific Highway and the state of Liechtenstein as security, I wrote him a cheque right there and then. Unlike the rest of Australia, I can understand his pain. He's got a fleet of jumbo jets and some islands in the South Pacific to maintain. And diamonds don't mine themselves.

The poor bloke hasn't got two bob to rub together for his space program. I mean, how can we expect Allan Moss to colonise Mars on a lousy thirty-three million a year?

And all this talk from the media is making me vomit. It's exceedingly poor form to kick a man when he's up.

These blokes work hard. Every morning Allan Moss is up at the crack of ten and he's a mere thirty grand to the good by the time he's scoffed down his Weeties.

Next it's off to work to check his emails, then out for a long lunch and a game of golf before he pops back into the office to make a few long-distance phone calls.

And he's a busy man. Well, he usually is. Right now, he's off work on a religious holiday. The Feast of Mammon, I think it is. He'll be off for a few days, feasting. But the moment the Feast of Mammon is over, and after the Festival of Covetousness, where merchant bankers covet one another's oxen for a week or two, he'll be right back to work.

Well actually no, then there's the Promulgation of Rapacity. That goes for a month but right after that he'll be back to work, doing what he does best: merchant banking and plenty of it. That's what merchant bankers do and Allan Moss does it better than anyone. And before you say it, merchant banking is not just rhyming slang.

Merchant banking is more than just a job. It's a way of life. It's not for everyone, and they don't let just anyone do it. You just can't walk into Macquarie Bank and ask to become a merchant banker. You have to be invited.

They asked me to join, and I attended one of their turns, which they conduct at a clandestine location at the stroke of midnight on the first Monday of every month. It's the first time I've had to put a blindfold on just to go and have a few drinks since I got on the turps with Tony Mokbel. They have a secret handshake – you have to do a few somersaults, a twist and a half pike before you actually press the other bloke's palm. I could show it to you but then I'd have to kill you.

There's a lot of fire, everyone's got a purple cloak on and after a while they bring in a goat dressed in a French maid's outfit. The moment the goat, whom the merchant bankers call 'Reg the Exalted One', enters the room, the bankers all hit the deck and start chanting over and over. Then you hit the turps and the bankers drone on and on about interest rates, bond yields, private equity buyouts and world domination. Everyone has to avert their gaze while the goat wanders around chewing on whatever he can get his teeth on but I managed to sneak a peek every now and then. He's a good-looking goat, Reg the Exalted One. A real class act. And the bankers think they'd be buggered without him.

By then I'd realised that merchant banking isn't the type of caper I could really stretch myself in. I liked the goat and think he'd be a tremendous dinner companion but I found the whole thing a bit fruity for my tastes. I'd rather stick knitting needles in my eyes than spend a night talking with bankers about interest rates, price/equity ratios and their bloody investment strategies.

Because that's where the merchant bankers get it wrong. It's not all about making a few bob. Look at poor old Mossy. He's pulling in thirty-three million a year, and still he's tapping me for a free lunch and a loan. And once a month he's on his knees, genuflecting to a bloody goat. Still no-one knows or cares who he is.

Meanwhile there are millions of kiddies around the country who go to sleep at night looking at posters on their walls of gangsta rappers and drug-addled sports stars who make truck loads more than Allan Moss. And these blokes don't have the common decency to get on their knees when Reg the Exalted One walks in the room.

Allan Moss: how's he supposed to colonise Mars on a lousy 33 mil a year?

Me and Richy Branson

I've known Richard Branson since he was pimply-faced, awkward naif. Way back then, Branson, sporting a pair of short pants and knitted vest, approached me and told me he wanted to start a company. He just couldn't think of the right name. I looked him up and down and said, 'Virgin, son' and Branson was away.

I've helped Richy out with a few tax problems over the years and he's heavily indebted to me. So in August last year, he offered me a drive into deep space on his *Virgin SpaceShipOne*. I didn't have to pay a zac. Richy flicked me a free ticket for the test-drive and he even let me invite a few friends along for the ride.

So I brought a few mates of mine from the Australian Cricket Team. I managed to convince the ACB the trip would be a valuable training exercise for the 2006 Ashes campaign. There was the skipper Ricky Ponting, Shane Warne, Glenn McGrath and Andy Symonds. Adam Gilchrist was invited to come along too but umpire Darrell Hair pinched his suit back at Virgin central command and stowed away. What with the helmet and all I didn't know Hairy was on board until we'd left the stratosphere.

Anyway, that morning we showed up at Coolangatta Airport, Richy pulled the rubber band back as far as it would go, counted back from 10 to 1, and let rip, flinging us into deep space, beyond the moon.

With the pre-flight nerves I'd had a few schooners of crème de menthe from the drinks trolley. We were in zero g's so I had to drink them through a straw. I know I shouldn't have been drinking and flying a spaceship and I don't want to condone that to the kiddies. If you drink and fly a spaceship, you're a bloody idiot, but I figured the coppers weren't likely to pick me up out here, so I'd be all right to get home.

From what I could see, I can tell you that space is kind of dark and really, really big.

Afterwards all sorts of people asked me to describe the magnificence of the spectacle, but I'm embarrassed to say, I don't really know. Once we hurtled through the atmosphere on Richy's burner, the boys got a bit excited, trying to pick out their homes from space, but when they got tired of that, they insisted we close the curtains and put the in-flight movie on. It was *Star Trek IV: The Voyage Home*.

I have to say that Star Trek space burner had a lot more going for it than *Virgin SpaceShipOne*. Lots more space for carry-on luggage, for a start.

Warney tried to bring a couple of hundred tins of baked beans but he got knocked back at Customs. The most they let him on board with was four cans and he wolfed them down through a straw. I'm just glad he kept the spacesuit on.

Andy Symonds got stuck into the duty-free grog before we even took off and passed out in his seat.

Poor old Warney hammered away on his phone with those massive fingers of his, trying to send a few SMS messages, but what with being several hundred thousand kilometres from the surface of Earth, he found he was out of range. He wasn't very happy about it and so he started harassing the hosties.

Warney told me that he wanted to be the first to join the 100,000-mile-high club but with the spacesuit on he was always going to struggle. He even tried to get a pizza delivered at one point. He's a great leg spin bowler but in all other respects, he's as dumb as a box of hair.

And speaking of Hair, Darrell was keeping an eye on Warney in case he took off to the brasco and got stuck into a bit of ball tampering.

Glenn McGrath was floating around pulling everyone's oxygen tubes out. He was the team practical jokester. But I told him enough's enough as he'd been getting right on my nerves. I told him if he didn't cut it out, I'd crash the spaceship into the back of Neptune. After that he quietened down a bit.

Meanwhile, Ricky Ponting took it upon himself to challenge David Boon's drinking record of fifty-three cans in a flight from Sydney to London. He was like a man possessed. It must be a Tasmanian thing. It was bloody near impossible in zero gravity, but Ricky's a fighter.

It all got a bit much for me after a while. I had the drinks trolley banging into the back of my head from the moment we left Earth and there was an in-flight meal – a chicken biryani that Warney couldn't stomach – floating about the place and getting stuck on the windscreen. The spaceship was a real mess and needed to be hosed out after re-entry. I couldn't have taken it back to Richy Branson in that state with a clear conscience.

Now some astronauts have said that flying in space became a religious experience for them. But the closest I got to that was thanking God that I'd never have to do this again. It's just like an intercontinental flight only longer and far more boring.

When we got back on the ground, I had a lot of explaining to do. Andy Symonds was unconscious, Warney had offended one of the trolley dollies and Glenn McGrath had opened a window with a penknife he smuggled on board. And back on Earth, one small step for Ricky Ponting – without him falling flat on his face – was nothing short of a bloody miracle.

I had to muck out Richy Branson's space burner all on my own. Just while I was mopping the sick off the ceiling, Richy himself walked in. I was terribly embarrassed but I didn't let on that the Ponting et al had been the culprits.

'Zero gravity played buggery with my guts, mate,' I told him. 'Sorright, Jack,' he said and grabbed a mop and started to help me out. 'You should have seen the mess I left in the Virgin Global Flyer balloon. Ten days without a brasco. It looked like Chuck Berry's bedroom by the time I'd finished.'

We both had a laugh and got on with the job. He's a good man Richy Branson and I'll always turn to him whenever I need a hand cleaning up vomit.

Richard Branson checks his spacesuit for signs of curry residue

CHAPTER EIGHT

The Law

It's Not Your Fault – Society's to Blame

The High Court

The highest court in the land was named the 'High Court' by someone with a passion for the bleeding obvious. When you appear before the High Court, you see a bunch of judges, perched up on a raised platform so they can look down at you. This makes your average justice look like a chemist at the back of a pharmacy. Odds are that he's fiddling around with a bottle of pills under the counter too. These boffins are housed in a building on the shores of Lake Burley Griffin that belongs to an architectural style called, I kid you not, 'the New Brutalism'. The horrible truth is that the whole thing was in fact constructed by a bunch of fat kids with a Meccano set.

Justice is Blind: ***She's Also Overweight, Drinks Heavily and is in an Abusive Relationship***
Traditionally, the High Court has been a useful place where a prime minister can park any irritating smart-arse minister who asks too many questions. They stay there, surrounded by a retinue of clerks and servants, until they turn seventy and hit the mandatory retirement age.

All too often these retired High Court justices are released into the community with no life skills whatsoever. Many are unable to dress themselves, let alone eat with a knife and fork.

Years ago I was pulled up on my way into a Canberra bottle shop by an old derro who threatened to kill me if I didn't stump up for his bus fare home. I thought, 'Bugger me, if that isn't Sir Garfield Barwick.'

Sure enough, the former chief justice had fallen on hard times after he hit the mandatory retirement age. I told Barwick I could never forgive him for his role in the Concrete Pipes case of 1971. But then I took pity on the poor bastard and gave him whatever lighter fluid I had on me and he moved on.

It's a disgrace that this nation's judicial heavyweights are cast out onto the streets at the tender age of seventy. I knew something had to be done when I saw old 'Bar' in a vomit-streaked dressing gown and slippers shuffling about outside the licensed grocer, putting his hand out for a few coins and a Viscount.

That's why I set up the first of the 'testimonials' in 1992. It provided a long overdue opportunity for retiring justices and chief justices to do a lap of honour and hold out an upturned wig to a grateful public. Back in those days, we had a piss-up in a panelbeating shop in Fyshwick, where a few girls I had on the books would get their kits off and we'd throw some money about on the Crown and Anchor.

Barwick: flung on the scrap heap by a nation that did not care

It's got bigger every year. A few years back, we moved it to the Mechanics' Institute in Queanbeyan for the extra space. Even so, this year we've had to knock back a couple of hundred punters from Ian Callinan's smoke night. And I hated doing it. God knows, 'Pie Guts' needs every cent we can pull together for him. The poor bastard could never survive on his earnings as a novelist.

Power Corrupts: *And the External Affairs Power Corrupts Absolutely*

The High Court was established by the constitution. The final draft of the constitution was written by Samuel Griffiths. No prize for guessing who the High Court's first chief justice was.

To begin with, the state governments enjoyed a fair suck of the sav when it came to sharing power with the Commonwealth. Then over time, more and more power accrued to the central government until all of Australia fell under the iron rule of a foul demon that men call Sauron the Unblinking Eye of Mordor, or the prime minister, as he's referred to in the papers.

The court handed stacks of power to the feds on a plate with a cherry on top through the misuse of some dodgy provisions in fine print, typed in up the back of the constitution. As a result, all a state government does these days is run an arts festival and appoint someone to ring Alan Jones in the morning and ask him what he wants this time.

Mabo A Go-Go

The Mabo case was easily the High Court's most important decision. After several years of heated debate, the court sat down and resolved that the Aboriginal people who were here when British settlers arrived were real and not a figment of the magic mushroom–inflamed imagination of Governor Phillip. Gritting their teeth, the court also agreed that Darth Vader was Luke Skywalker's father and that Rock Hudson was probably gay.

And so the court abolished the fiction that Australia was terra nullius: a Latin term which means 'there's nothing decent on the telly tonight'.

Aboriginal and Torres Strait Islander people cheered and nothing went wrong for them ever again.

The High Court's first sitting in 1903: Sammy Griffiths grabbed the big chair in the middle

The Court Today

Today the court is a lean, mean judgin' machine, tossing out sober judgements, witty judicial banter and steamy, erotic literature at a rate that proves the nay-sayers wrong yet again.

Sadly the wigs are gone.

They're wearing their smocks and they're ready for their finger painting. Then it's nap time.

IT'S A COMFORT THING

Like the justices of the High Court, the justices of the Federal Court have eschewed their horsehair wigs, believing that the wigs have no place in a modern judicial system. They continue to wear merkins, made from the finest goat hair, but say they do so strictly for personal reasons.

Know Your Justices

Chief Justice Murray Gleeson: Murray Gleeson is not a bloke given to overt acts of emotion. The poor bastard attempted smiling once, but the act caused him such pain that he doesn't dare repeat the feat, forcing him to be stuck with this deeply constipated expression ever since.

To his mates, though, Muzza is a top bloke and a whiz with the law. He fixed up the conveyancing on my beach house in five minutes flat and all it cost me was a slab of VB and a canned ham.

Justice Gummow: Billy Gummow's a smart bloke and the books behind him prove it: not only does he practise law, he's one hell of a reader as well. I've seen him knock over a Grisham novel in an afternoon. I don't know how he does it. I'd rather pour molten lead in my eyes than read Grisham.

Justice Kirby: Kirby calls himself a defender of the intellectually disabled, yet he is callously critical of Senator Bill Heffernan, a tragic victim of weird psychosexuality and animal husbandry who is simply unable to control his Tourette's-like ranting in the Senate. Have you no compassion, sir?

Justice Heydon: Don't let that stern visage fool you, Heydos is a very funny bugger. I've seen him do routines at smoke nights where I nearly pissed my pants. He once handed down a judgement while playing 'Give Me That Thing' on a moog synthesiser. The Rodney Dangerfield of the Full Bench.

Justice Crennan: A victim of affirmative action, Crennan was passed over several times for the High Court because of a perceived need to get more males on the bench. Once this anti-male bias was overcome, it was considered safe to appoint a sheila again and little Suzy was given the funny wig and fake bookshelf at last.

Justice Hayne: Frankly, I don't know much about this bloke. Many court watchers suspect that Hayne was never actually appointed to the High Court. I think Haynesy just showed up one day with a briefcase in his hand and security let him in. To his credit, he's turned up every day ever since.

Justice Kiefel: The newbie, her appointment to the High Court commenced in September 2007, following the retirement of Justice Callinan. Just fifty-two years of age, Susan Kiefel will be sitting on the High Court for the next eighteen years before she has to give it away. You don't get that long for murder.

Your Problems Solved

Problem: Your husband is a senior legal figure with a filthy secret life.
Solution: Threaten to expose his fetish for lying in public urinals in a Girl Guide costume to *tout le monde*!
Method: Remind him, gently but *firmly*, that he is *not* a man of independent wealth and that if his secret was exposed, he would suddenly find himself *utterly bereft* of status, of wherewithal and friends, other than those who dwell in the squalid *demi-monde* he currently inhabits. I hope I'm making myself perfectly clear, dear.
Result: Marital bliss, dear reader!

When the Law Isn't Enough

Every now and then a government will scan the social landscape, do a quick headcount and determine that there's not nearly enough folk in the slammer. They could dispatch the plod in divvy vans and round up some undesirables but there was always the problem: what to charge them with? That's when any government worth its salt realises it needs to bang out a few new laws.

But judges don't like new laws. They've gone to a lot of trouble to learn all the old ones. The laws come in lots of really big books without pictures in them. It's a lot of hard work to read them, let alone remember them, and when some bugger wants to tack bits on, the judges become very confused and need to take a long lie-down.

In 2005, Federal Attorney-General Philip Ruddock hit on a solution. Phil decided to leave judges out of the process altogether. He got the young kiddie on work experience to write up a bill which would circumvent judicial process and give the police the powers they'd been demanding for years. Phil set himself up as judge and jury. If he wasn't in, his receptionist would grab the gavel and take on the job.

The bill got through the House of Reps after a gruelling ten-minute rant from Phil, followed by a quick round of back slapping from the opposition. The bill went to the Senate and got the thumbs up. A courier dropped it off in a manilla envelope at Yarralumla that afternoon and when Governor-General Michael Jeffery scrawled his moniker on it, it was passed into law as the *Anti-Terrorism Act 2005*. At last everyone was happy.

Troublemakers and angry loners all over the country were given a lift in a divvy van and a new brown track suit to wear. Some of them had been playing with crackers and eyeing off landmarks, like the Big Prawn in Exmouth, so they knew it was a fair cop.

Phil's bill has been such a success that most young blokes who've been playing with crackers, thinking of playing with crackers, associating with blokes who've been playing with crackers, or associating with blokes thinking of playing with crackers or urging other blokes to buy crackers, now know the jig is up and report to the nearest police station at their earliest convenience, pop on a brown track suit and take what's coming to them.

And if that weren't enough, Phil knocked out a fridge magnet that calmed a panicked nation with its warming ferromagnetism, took the fight up to the terrorists and reinstated the refrigerator as the primary communicative white good in the home. Australians owe Phil Ruddock a great debt in my view. If it were down to me, I'd give him a ride in a divvy van and a brown track suit right now.

The Courts and Freedom of Speech

The court system in this country exists only to further the political interests of the Liberals through the defamation laws. This is an incontrovertible fact. I have been picked up and dashed upon the rocks of these laws time and time again and I am poorer by hundreds of thousands of dollars as a result.

Let me give you just two examples, comrade.

In my memoir (*The Howard Years and Why You Should Kill Yourself*, Random House Australia, 1998), I wrote that ***** had only become Liberal leader because ***** had fucked ***** before she discovered that ***** when stroked vigorously with a large collapsible ****** was much more to her liking.

In 1995 I wrote an op-ed piece in the *Herald* where I denounced a rumour circulating at the time that former Prime Minister ***** had fathered a bastard child upon ****** in a urine-stained *****. I said the whole thing was a disgusting fabrication and I knew it to be so because I had witnessed **** with ***** from a hole in the wall of my motel room and I knew of her strong moral objections to ***** with **** and several tattooed ******. Therefore, I valiantly concluded, conceiving a child by this man was, for her, an utter impossibility. Even if he was, by and large, the erotic cesspit that his enemies claimed him to be.

For my defence of this man's character, I was found guilty of having somehow defamed him by Justice ***** of the New South Wales Supreme Court – a man who closely resembles a curled lip in a wig. Amidst all the questions of how and where and why, no-one bothered to ask who. *Cui bono*?

And lo it came to pass that I was compelled to attend court for many months and so when summoned to late-night drinks at the Lodge I could not go and I did not advise Paul to fund a national theatre company for ongoing performance of my work and my trilogy of plays about the perfidy of the Liberals was not staged and the populace were not alerted to their hatefulness and Paul lost the election and Howard was duly elected by the ignorant masses who knew not what they were doing and the bright clear sky of hope was darkened and the curtain was rent in two and we walked from the Temple weeping and clutching at our hair for we knew that that evil pederast on the bench had planned it all along.

Prove I lie.

The Cash, the Bash and the Gash

It's become almost de rigueur to knock the cops in Australia. Maybe that's why they're so good at returning the favour.

I recall raising this very topic with Roger 'The Dodger' Rogerson over a sweet and sour, 112 schooners and some incredibly dexterous Asian girls. 'Rog,' I said to him, 'How come you blokes are despised and mistrusted by the public?' Roger just looked me in the eye and smiled. Then he took me down to Darlo Police Station and gave me a good kicking.

Australian cops aren't big on self analysis. And they don't brook much criticism. Personally, I don't blame them for being a bit testy. The poor buggers are constantly having to deal with a bunch of prying do-gooders looking over their shoulders, asking them a lot of impertinent questions about fundamental human rights, reasonable cause and why that bloke in the cells isn't moving.

The Dodger took criminals off the streets and out for a spot of lunch

Left to their own devices, Australian coppers have proven to be tremendously effective in solving crime while keeping a bit of time free to show off their entrepreneurial talents. Men of action like Ray Kelly, Fred Krahe, Graham 'Chook' Fowler and the Dodger himself have taken hundreds of violent criminals off the streets, taken them to lunch and confiscated the proceeds of their nefarious activities.

In Queensland, Terry Lewis, while not terribly heroic as such, nevertheless got the job done and kept prostitutes off the streets so they'd have plenty of energy when they got to Russ Hinze's place on a Wednesday night.

In Victoria, the Drug Squad very sensibly decided to take an holistic approach to fighting crime; at least that's what they said they were doing when they got pinched with all those drugs.

The commentariat can slag off at the coppers until they choke on their haughty verbiage but you won't find me joining them. You won't find me calling for costly and intrusive royal commissions and other nosy inquiries because I understand just how valuable the bulls are to have around. And just what can happen if, for some reason, they decide to pull the pin.

AUSTRALIA'S POLICE MOTTOS

It is a matter of regret that the nation's police forces have determined to ditch their Latin mottos in favour of something in English that's warm and cuddly but doesn't really get to the core of their work. What the police need is new Latin mottos, so Latin scholars can determine in a trice just who they're dealing with.

NEW SOUTH WALES

Illic nusquam ultum nos operor

(There's nothing much we can do)

In the wake of the Wood Royal Commission, the New South Wales police force is now virtually corruption free. Most New South Wales coppers are on leave at any given time and are working hard on their second and third jobs; usually as nightclub bouncers. This leaves little time for actual police work, so when you call to report a crime, they'll ask your name and address and then tell you they have no intention of going out to make further inquiries. Besides, by the time they get there, it'll be all over anyway, right?

QUEENSLAND

Invado pax, amicus

(Get in the truck, pal)

The motto is a stout reminder that the Queensland police don't take any guff from anyone, ever. You'd better do as you're asked. So what if you didn't do anything wrong? That's for the courts to decide – and the Queensland police might just tell a few porkies in court to get a conviction. Ever heard of any Queensland copper being charged with perjury? It doesn't happen.

SOUTH AUSTRALIA

Quis et nidor?

(What's that smell?)

South Australia's police force is poorly resourced, leading to the use of junior officers instead of cadaver-detecting dogs. Human olfactory capacities are about one-hundredth of a canine's, leading many junior officers to make this speculative exclamation while sniffing around old banks and shallow graves. Happily, they usually find a corpse or two.

TASMANIA

Vos iustus evanui quod nemo vel teneo vos erant absentis

(You could just disappear and no-one would even know you were missing)

The Apple Isle is a big place with few people and the Tasmanian police will not let you forget it. Best off tell them what they want to know, even if you have to make it up.

VICTORIA

Illud modo intercipiam

(I'll just put this in my pocket for now)

Happily VicPol has plenty of time on its hands after a sharp decline in underworld personnel in recent times. Victorian coppers haven't been idle though and have spent plenty of time concentrating on confiscating gear from what's left of the criminal population. Every day you can see the Victorian wallopers walking in and out of houses with plasma tellies and jet skis, grinning their arses off. The biggest problem is where to put it all. But VicPol is nothing if not inventive.

WESTERN AUSTRALIA

Ego volo vos reputo ut aurum est vestry

(I suppose you think that gold bullion is yours)

Western Australia's Crime and Corruption Commission has exposed a certain moral laxity in some of its serving officers. Due to rocketing real estate prices in Western Australia, they're eminently bribable.

THE AFP

Patriam ab ipsa tutara

(Protecting Australia from itself)

Grown from a bunch of grey bombers, shuffling around the streets of Canberra handing out parking tickets in the 1970s to the lean, mean anti-terrorist machine they are today. Can arrest people and detain them for as long as they want, which is handy if there's nothing to charge them with. Able to shut entire cities down at a moment's notice, so they can jump out of choppers and generally skylark about.

THE VICTORIAN POLICE STRIKE OF 1923

Corruption Takes a Holiday and All Hell Breaks Loose

In Victoria back in 1923, the cops had had a gutful of having their methods questioned and promptly went on strike.

The plod hadn't downed tools for more than a few hours before the first window at Myers got smashed and people started helping themselves to a bit of gear. The following night it was on for young and old: full-scale looting. In the absence of law enforcement, the fabric of Australian society had been rent apart in less than forty-eight hours.

The prime minister, Stanley Bruce, was a trembling heap. Bruce was a whimpering, genuflecting Anglophile; a worthless shill, hurled into the spotlight by some perverse electoral parapraxis. And now that power had fallen into his lap, he was in a state of almost permanent political quadriplegia at the thought of losing it.

On the night of the coppers' strike, it was clear that he had crossed the line and was marching right on into terminal psychosis territory. Bruce was sitting sobbing on a divan in the Royal Suite of the Windsor Hotel, dressed in a red and black satin evening gown, toying distractedly with a string of pearls. He was utterly alone, aside from his wife, Ethel, his five senior staff members and a border collie named Sparkie.

That's when a young Bob Menzies, in his first year as a state parliamentarian, strode into the room and told them all to get out. When they left, Bob grabbed Bruce by his plunging neckline and slapped him hard across the face. 'You idiot, this is Australia,' he told the puling moron, 'The entire nation will be ablaze by Wednesday. For God's sake man, call in the troops.'

That craven left-footer Bruce just didn't get it, but Menzies was a country kid and he understood instinctively that Australians will get stuck right into a bit of crime if they think the coppers are looking the other way.

Prime Minister Stanley Bruce: a fawning Anglophile and appalling deviant who quite rightly got the arse in the 1929 election

It has always been thus. Australians won't mess about, given the opportunity. There may be a pause to contemplate the moral dimension, but then we come to our senses and help ourselves to that plasma screen TV. Which was just sitting there. And if we didn't knock it off, then someone else would.

Anyway, in the end Menzies had to belt Bruce senseless before he finally gave in and reached for the phone.

With the green machine on the streets, things calmed down in no time. Mindful of the prospect of a little small-calibre crowd control, the populace quickly fell back into line and popped off to the cricket for the afternoon.

But the army couldn't hang about shooting wildly in all directions. They had other things to do. So the politicians reluctantly turned to the coppers, and begged them to get back to work.

The coppers had made the ultimate sacrifice – getting on the drink and staying off work for a couple of days. And it paid off. They were reinstated with better pay and conditions. And the best thing was their interrogators – the toecutters and spooks – were all given the flick. So no worries, eh?

The great legacy of the strike of 1923 was that the cops had won the first important battle in the war for self-regulation and thus ensured that honest coppers in Australia are like Papuan porn stars. You don't see many of them about.

And I'm here to tell you that it's a whole lot easier dealing with bent coppers than honest ones. They're the only ones who can keep a bit of fuckin' order around the place. And that's why it makes sense to pony up with a few bob just to keep them keen. So next time you get pulled over, smile – try and be polite and reach for your wallet. Think of it as a gift from a grateful public.

Even coppers need to feel valued.

POSITIONS VACANT

Do you have what it takes?

MELBOURNE CRIME SCENE

Due to some unexpected internal demotions, the Melbourne Crime Scene is seeking energetic, fun-loving people to join its ever-expanding network. We are looking for self-motivated individuals with previous experience and a genuine interest in the debt collection, pharmaceutical and adult entertainment sectors.

Do you possess the following attributes?

If you think you've got what it takes, the Melbourne Crime Scene would like to speak to you

PLEASE FORWARD YOUR RÉSUMÉ TO:
Carl Williams c/– Department of Corrections, Victoria
OR:
Stuff it into a tennis ball and hurl it over the wall of 'B' Block, Port Phillip Correctional Centre, Laverton, VIC

CHAPTER NINE

Religion

I've Tried Them All, So You Don't Have To

Religion in Australia: A Spiritual Smorgasbord

Since I hit forty, I've felt the need to grapple with something much larger than myself. Most of the time I can service that need with an oversized Queensland sheila I call Cyclone Beryl. But sometimes it's not enough. And that's when I come over all spiritual.

I'm on my own quest for meaning. So over the years whenever I've run into a religious leader (and I've run into some of them in the strangest places), I tell him to leave the boy scout alone for a bit and give me some insight into what his crew are all about. Each of the great religions has its own traditions, its own view of the universe and, most importantly, its own sphere of influence.

But which religion to pick? Which one will give you the right amount of spiritual nourishment? And if you sign up, can you still get a drink and a root?

I've had a crack at all of them at one time or another. Here's a digest of everything you need to know.

The Catholics

It may come as a surprise to many to learn that I am a practising Catholic. Roman Catholics like a drink and a punt and I am drawn to the religion on that basis alone. I also find the church's habit of looking blankly into the distance in the face of bizarre sexual conduct to be most refreshing.

I have enormous respect for Australia's leading tyke, Cardinal Georgie Pell; he's a back-to-basics-no-nonsense-get-fucked-if-you-don't-like-it kind of man.

Georgie remains intensely focused on the teachings of Christ – none of that crap about turning the other cheek, judge not others, etc. George is much more interested in the specific prohibitions Jesus gave against frangers, stem cell research and the Gay Mardi Gras.

The tykes came to Australia on the First Fleet and spent the first 150 years here crying about Ireland.

The prots were the top of the heap for a long, long time and us Catholics pretty much had to cop it sweet.

Name	Catholic Church
Deity	The Holy Trinity: a triple-deck creation machine that includes Yahweh, the god of the Hebrews, Jesus of Nazareth and the Holy Spirit.
Leader	The Pope. Named after the Popemobile, the novelty car that drives him around football stadiums.
Holy Book	The Holy Bible, written in Latin, chiselled into the fabric of your immortal soul.
Can you get a drink?	Is the Pope Catholic? It's practically compulsory with this crowd.
Can you get a root?	No, with an 'if', and yes, with a 'but'.

It was during World War I that Catholics started to show some political muscle. There was a shortage of volunteers so the PM Billy Hughes wanted to force young men onto the battlefields of France at the tip of a bayonet. Hughes had never fought in a war himself, but was dead keen to get others to fight on the other side of the world. Which is almost the same thing.

Archbishop Daniel Mannix led demonstrations in the streets against conscription and the whole thing fell over. Mannix was hugely influential in the Labor Party at the time and people began to grumble that the ALP was a Catholic conspiracy. They were half right: Mannix was running a conspiracy, but it was one that split the ALP from arsehole to breakfast-time when he discovered the ALP didn't hate communism as vehemently as he would have liked.

Daniel Mannix: a man so humble he used to make his own hats with a broken kite and some horsehair

For decades, Australia was split along sectarian lines. If your dad worked in the Treasury he was a Freemason; if he worked in the Taxation Department he was a Catholic. If he barracked for Carlton he was C of E; if it was Collingwood he was a left-footer. If your dad was done for fraud he was a prot; if it was armed robbery, he was a tyke. Everyone knew where they stood.

The old sectarianism ended in the sixties and attendance at mass sharply declined along with it. And no wonder; nowadays on a Sunday morning you can choose between kneeling in a draughty stone pile or sitting in front of the TV, making the front of your pyjamas dance while you watch Christina Aguilera on *Video Hits*. It's not a difficult decision to make.

The Bible – A Heretic's Guide

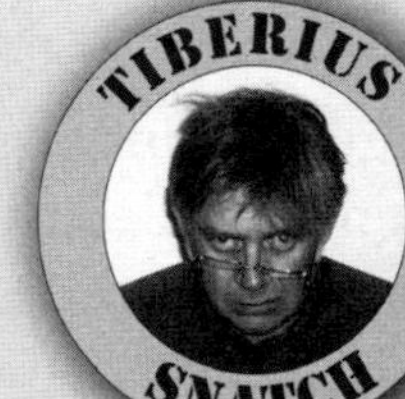

Gentle reader, I was raised as a Presbyterian and I spent much of those mad summer months of my adolescence in Bible camp studying the old and new testaments. The simple verities of my faith were untroubled until a bright morning in 1960 when I beheld the splendid form of the host of Channel Seven's *Romper Room* and lo, my loins turned rigid with excitement. As my adolescent body became alive to the...

Again it seems I must leave off here at the insistence of my publishers who advise me that inclusion of excerpts from my sexual diaries of 1960–75 are 'really, really' inappropriate. It really makes one wonder why one was invited to contribute in the first place. So it's goodbye to Germaine and your haughty gaze; goodbye to Jackie and your thighs that could crack walnuts with their feral strength; farewell Beatrice and Helen. Alas, those memories are now destined to remain unrecorded, and to simply disappear, like teardrops in the cold, cold drizzle of this new moral climate.

It's all been deleted from my hard drive. Is everyone happy now?

Jack Inside the Vatican

With the untimely demise of Pope John Paul II, the world turned to Rome to see who would be the next bloke to be carried about in a sedan chair. I received an urgent call from the Vatican, asking me to fly over and scrutinise the papal election; y'know, set up the closed-circuit cameras in the basilica and just generally keep an eye on things.

The election of the Pope by the College of Cardinals is shrouded in mystery and intrigue for outsiders, infidels and non-believers but I am here to tell you that it is a simple thing and one in which the hand of God can easily be seen.

The cardinals assemble in the Sistine Chapel and after a quick three-hour mass, rip off their cassocks. Whoever is the most hirsute gets the gig. It is as simple as that. Of course, John Paul II was more ape than man and easily accounted for his opponents in 1979.

On 19 April Year of Our Lord 2005, with the very hairy John Paul II gone to God, the cardinals met to exchange bodily fluids and compare physiques. I would note firstly that our local boy, Big Georgie Pell, is in possession of a stunning physique, as if chiselled from granite, but alas, nary a hair, pubic or otherwise, is in evidence. I can say only that he will have to put in some very hard work before the next election.

Anyway, on that day, it all came down to Cardinal Arinze, a Hottentot from Nigeria, and the German, Joey Ratzinger. Arinze had plaited his back hair with some very colourful beads but many thought this a cheap and tawdry attempt to clamber into St Peter's throne. There was a general hubbub concerning Arinze's back dreads but when Cardinal Ratzinger thrust his left arm forward to silence the assembly, things changed dramatically. At first I thought Ratzinger had strapped an otter to his shoulder, such was the thick mat of hair on view. But on a second glance I knew this was no prop, the hair was all Joey, and from there he had the pontificate in the bag. Once the penny dropped with the rest of the cardinals, one of the girls there set fire to a couple of copies of the *Women's Weekly* and then the rest of the world knew what we did: *Habemus Papam*. We have a Pope.

Joe Ratzinger is accused of holding some views that some may find a little fruity. I will admit he knows fuck-all about the greyhounds and his knowledge of Australian Rules football is scant at best. On the day after he was given the gig, I spent the day with him in front of a giant-screen TV, punting on the gees goin' around at a midweek meet at the Sha Tin racecourse in Hong Kong. He was punting like a madman on his phone account and, in the strictest confidence, let me tell you Benedict XVI, Our Pope, is one of the worst punters I've seen.

You'd think he'd get the best tips going, wouldn't you? Calls from the Khashoggis, Dermot Weld and Bart Cummings, every hour on the hour.

Pope Benedict XVI: a top bloke but his scant knowledge of footy will always hold him back

The truth is Our Pope gets very little decent mail. He tends to punt according to some overly complicated algorithmic equation I still don't understand. I kept trying to tell him that punting wasn't a numbers game; it was all about which horse was on the best juice and which corrupt dwarf would beat it shitless as it went around. But do you think Benedict XVI would listen? Get fucked, he would. He did his nuts, losing three cathedrals in Venezuela before getting out of jail with a fluke trifecta at the Sandown dogs later that day.

God's Pit Bull Terrier may be a shithouse punter, but he's a decent bloke; quick with a shout, generous to a fault, excellent after-dinner company and a real man's man.

The Pope's detractors point to his days with the Hitler Youth as a blemish on his character, but that's a bit rich. Look, Joey played for the wrong team back then, there's no doubt about it. But it's hardly Joey's fault if Pius XII used to look the other way as the trains went past way back during World War II.

Joey was just a boy when all that was going on. He turned eighteen three weeks before the war in Europe ended. Joey has said that he never fired a shot from the 8-millimetre howitzer anti-aircraft gun he was trained to use at sixteen. You'd think he must've let rip once to see how much noise it made. But he's said he didn't and I'm not inclined to mistrust popes off the bat.

Truth is of course, by 1944, the Nazis had put a lot of kiddies like Joe Ratzinger in the twos, given them a run off the bench and told them if they didn't go hard, they'd be hanging out of a tree by lunchtime. It was not a good time to put your hand in the air and ask to be excused.

Joey and his brother, Georg, headed off to a seminary, mitres on their bonces and hit the books with Europe still smouldering. Both lads popped the frock on in 1951. According to their mum, Maria, they both seemed to have found their niche in the Catholic Church but 'Joey really took to it.'

By 1985, Joey Ratzinger had kicked on to become a cardinal.

More ominously, Ratzinger held the title of 'The Grand Inquisitor of Mother Rome', and alongside the hirsute John Paul II, he stomped on heresy wherever it appeared, thus ensuring that Catholic theology has remained within the jurisdiction of a very workable committee of a handful of old blokes in Rome.

Ratzinger's important theological works have directly challenged all manner of seditious discussion raised by churlish and irresponsible priests who'd prefer to bow and scrape to Fidel Castro than kneel before God. Ratzinger's two most noted works, highlighting the role of women in Catholicism, 'Clean my house before I get back' and 'Fix me a sandwich, already', are considered invaluable spiritual guides to those who struggle to hear the voice of truth in the modern religious world, namely women.

On all counts Benedict XVI, Our Pope, is the man for the job. We must embrace our new Papa. He is a fine man, none finer in my book, and certainly one to watch when it comes time to take the Roman Catholic Church back to the fourteenth century, where, frankly, it belongs.

The Anglicans

Name	Anglican Church of Australia
Deity	Same as the Catholics, but, y'know, nicer.
Leader	One of the world's leading agnostics, the Archbishop of Canterbury
Holy Book	*Tales of Beatrix Potter*
Can you get a drink?	Ooh! Just half a glass of sherry, thank you.
Can you get a root?	What? Why do you ask?! What have you heard!? What!?

This lot have seriously lost their bottle, but they used to be hugely impressive back in the sixteenth century. The whole caper got started because Henry VIII was sick of Catherine of Aragon's truculent inability to produce a male heir, and the Catholics refused him a divorce. He was left with no alternative: he set up a whole new church, ordered everyone to get in, and if anyone was lingering outside he put a flaming sword in their innards. All that so he didn't have to put up with the wife's snooty bullshit.

Henry VIII was a wild man and a fat bearded bastard but he was a man of action and a bloody good drinker. He was the Damir Dokić of his time and I salute him for that.

In years gone by the Church of England in Australia was the Liberal Party at prayer. Back in the good old days, the best way to get a mining lease in WA was to sort it out with the premier over a cup of tea and a Monte Carlo behind the hot-water urn after the service.

These days, the whole thing has gone to heck in a hand basket. The Anglicans are split in Australia between the 'High' and 'Low' church. The High Church is based in Melbourne and Adelaide. This lot want to be Catholics but they're worried they'll be kicked out of the Melbourne Club. Homosexuals are admitted on a don't-tell-don't-ask basis. (As in 'Don't tell the vicar you're gay because he might ask you out for a drink at the Peel.')

The Low Church is based in Sydney and it's a completely different beast. This crowd hate the smells and bells of the wannabe Catholics down south. They've got a hardcore commitment to scriptural integrity and wearing seriously ugly clothes. Like the High Church, they're obsessed with homosexuality. They say 'love the sinner, hate the sin', but in their hearts they do enjoy making poofters feel like shit.

The Archbishop of Canterbury, Dr Rowan Williams: a ruthless dictator who seeks to intimidate dissenters by the power of his eyebrows alone

The Muslims

'Islam' is a word that simply means 'obedience'. It means submitting to that little voice inside your head; the one that is telling me right now to put down my pen and move slowly away from the desk.

Ayman al-Zawahiri: a tremendous bloke and, more importantly, not a man to harbour a grudge

Name	Islam
Deity	Allah, the Most Merciful. Merciful. I said Merciful.
Leader	That very nice man who succeeded Sheik Hilali.
Holy Book	The Koran. It's a top read. It really makes you think.
Can you get a drink?	I'm really not thirsty, thanks all the same.
Can you get a root?	Look, I really think we need to move on. In my view there has been far too much focus on the perceived shortcomings of Islam. The truth is, it's a tremendous religion full of lovely people who wouldn't hurt a fly. Or an author. A simple man given to occasional outbursts of thoughtlessness and stupidity for which he would like to apologise here and now. So no hard feelings, eh? I mean who am I to say what's good about Islam or Mohammed. Oh shit, I mentioned his name. Sorry. Sorry . . .

The Problem with Islam

Let me make myself perfectly clear: I hold no problem with a woman in a headscarf hiding her particulars from the rest of the world. And if Abdul wants to slide out five times a day to pray towards Mecca, good bloody luck to him. And the World Trade Center? Well them Muslims should never have copped the blame for that one: that was actually caused by a cabal of Giant Yellow Lizards working in disguise in the duty-free shops at JFK International Airport. The proof is on my website. Check it out.

The thing that really gives me shits is the beard: the beard with no moustache. What the fuck is that? That looks a bit fucken weird doesn't it, eh?

And that brings me to the problem with Muslims in this country: they don't fit in. They don't participate.

I myself belong to several public-spirited organisations and there's not a bearded carpet botherer who bothers to show up for any of them.

Let me give you an example: I've been president of the Henley Beach Thomas the Tank Engine Adult Appreciation Society here in Adelaide for six, no, I tell a lie – for seven years now. And when has a Muslim showed up at a meeting?

NEVER. That's how often.

My chapter of Narcotics Anonymous declares a heroin-free day at the kiddies' playground around the corner, and does anyone called Mohammed or Saddam or Osama show up to help? They do not.

Instead it was left to the regular blokes. Blokes with normal names like Chook, Wazza and Boof. Well Boof had to leave after he spilled bong water on a six-year-old, but that's better than nothing, isn't it? Where's the civic participation? Where's the public spirit from the beard and towel set?

Paul Sheehan's right: the problem with Muslims is they come here in boats, they have too many kids and they're beholden to foreign religious leaders. Of course this used to be said about Irish Catholics like Sheehan, and they were right about those Papist Lizard-worshipping idolaters too.

I've given this a great deal of thought and I think it can be said that the Muslim world is like a great big giant humungous Holden Barina. Think about it. The wheels are like jihad, powering them down the road to who-knows-where. The windscreen wipers are the moderates, fighting desperately to give them some clarity of vision. The engine is like . . . like . . . The engine, that's like the oil, which powers their armies! No, hang on, the oil goes in the engine. Shit, I'll get back to you on that one.

Anyway you see my point. Keep this country free and safe for normal people. Like me.

This is an image of the prophet Mohammed. Or maybe it isn't. In simple bricks and mortar terms, Mohammed did nothing for the development of Australia.

The Judaists

Name	Judaism
Deity	Y*hw*h
Leader	Henny Youngman
Holy Book	*Portnoy's Complaint*
Can you get a drink?	Yes, but only at bar mitzvahs and weddings.
Can you get a root?	Yes, but it involves a lot of begging and pleading.

Like the Catholics, the Red Sea pedestrians also arrived here on the First Fleet, and they've contributed enormously to Australian life for better or worse. It could be said that General Sir John Monash and Isaac Isaacs have paid off the karmic debt inflicted by Austen Tayshus, but karma is a Buddhist precept, and the Jewish god is way more fun than that tedious Indian wowser.

I've always had a soft spot for Yahweh, the god of the Hebrews. Anyone who could destroy Sodom and Gomorrah on a hangover, and who could cover Job in weeping sores in a bet with the devil, is tops in my book.

When the shit comes raining down, the goyim whine and want to know why the world isn't perfect. Jews have the Torah and they know that if there is a god, he's barking mad. Or on the piss. He definitely has a sense of humour. How else would you explain anthrax, tuberculosis and the National Party?

Around four thousand years ago, God told the Jewish people that they were his chosen people. After centuries of persecution, pogroms and the Holocaust, many of them began to ask, 'Chosen for what?'

There was some talk about setting up a Jewish homeland somewhere in Australia. It was never made official but it came into being anyway. The homeland was called 'Caulfield' and a kosher butcher and a cake shop were set up to commemorate its establishment.

Grand final day in 1966 fell on Yom Kippur, the Day of Atonement. Every Jew in Melbourne was praying for a St Kilda victory and they beat Collingwood by a single point. This was taken as proof that God is Jewish, which was true, but even he couldn't get into the Melbourne Club at the time.

Today the Jewish community in Australia is seriously split between those who think Ariel Sharon was a terrific humanitarian (the so-called Nazi Jews) and those who think Hamas should be given a fair shake in the West Bank (the so-called Self-Hating Jews). Then there are the Orthodox types who reckon Israel shouldn't be there in the first place. And there are the out-and-out extremists who think that Woody Allen is a seriously overrated filmmaker who hasn't made a decent flick since *Bananas*.

The Buddhists

Name	Buddhism
Deity	Prince Siddhartha Gautama, the enlightened one
Leader	Bretty Kirk
Holy Book	Various sutras and canons and *The Secret* by Rhonda Byrne
Can you get a drink?	No. You're expected to refrain from intoxicants, which gives rise to 'mindlessness'. I thought that was the whole point of the thing, but there you go.
Can you get a root?	No, and why would you want one when they shave their heads like that? I knocked back Sinéad O'Connor a few times. Why would I give one of these sheilas a go?

Buddhism is taking off in Australia right now. But under no circumstances should you go to the track with a Buddhist. No matter what the race outcome is, they'll just shrug their shoulders and claim the result was always meant to be thus. If that's true, then why the fuck didn't you speak up before the race started when I was in the queue at the bookie's?

Your average Buddhist attempts to replicate the 'awakening' of the Buddha, Prince Siddhartha Gautama. Siddhartha's journey to enlightenment began with great material wealth. Then he chose a life of poverty, cleaning car windows on street corners with a bottle of Windex and a bucket. Finally he hit upon the Middle Way, somewhere in between.

The spiritual home for many Buddhists is Tibet. While the Chinese have moved in and knocked up a few Noodle Kings for the punters, I'm not entirely convinced that they have the best interests of the Tibetan people at heart.

I say give the place back to the Tibetans. Maybe then they'll build a decent duty-free shop at Lhasa Airport. I hope so, because the current one is a disgrace. There isn't a Ken Done jumper in sight and the place smells to buggery of sandalwood.

Like the Hindus and the Jainists, Buddhists believe in the concept of karma, which basically means what goes around comes around. And that particularly applies to certain craven little bastards who dob in a mate; a mate who had very little to do with a certain racing scandal. Trevor, if you're reading this, Buddha tells me you're in for a clip across the ear sometime soon.

Me and the Dalai Lama: Some Days are Robeses

I'm not ashamed to admit that I met with the Dalai Lama when he was here recently, unlike some others I could mention, namely the political leadership of this country.

Johnnie Howard had been telling anyone who cared to listen that he'd lost his diary so he couldn't make a time to see the Dalai Lama as it might have clashed with an important appointment he may have made with the beautician to get his eyebrows sandblasted.

Poor old Kevvy Rudd. It's not that he doesn't like the Dalai Lama, it's just that upsetting the Chinese is anathema to him. So he took the easy way out and met the Dalai over a cup of tea and a Milk Arrowroot. But Kevvy only smiled politely and didn't actually say a word to the Dalai and the subject of Tibet certainly didn't get a mention.

I don't know what all the fuss is about. The Chinese Government gets angry with our politicians for having the temerity to have a chat with the Dalai Lama because they see the Dalai Lama as an unelected and dangerous world leader, answerable to no-one. They see it as some sort of demarcation dispute. You see, the Chinese Government reckon they've got dibs on dangerous, unaccountable leaders answerable to no-one.

The Dalai Lama: one of the wisest punters I've met

But it's nothing for our politicians to worry about: just a diplomatic tempest in a teacup. The Chinese just feign mock outrage for the next month or so before getting on with the serious business of carving out huge chunks of Australia and loading them on a jumbo, bound for Beijing.

While others lacked the courage to show the Dalai a bit of Australian hospitality, at least I showed a bit of manners and decided to take him out for a night on the tiles. I was going to take him to the races on Saturday but we were both a bit pushed for time and worried about Chinese spies, so I took him to the Caboolture RSL and we watched the races on the big-screen TVs and had an afternoon on the punt.

He's a very smart punter, the Dalai Lama. He's an each-way gambler as you might expect and while I dropped a couple of hundred, the Dalai broke even. We punted all day and all night until the Gold

Coast greyhounds packed it in for the night. The Dalai didn't win anything but he couldn't lose either. I was in awe of him.

Anyway, after the Caboolture RSL closed, we finished up in some rough nightclub on the coast. When we got there, there were two bikie gangs facing off over a turf war. You could have cut the tension with a knife and it would have been easy to do it because there were a lot of blokes there with knives.

Then the Dalai Lama stepped in and, within minutes, these monstrous bikies were hugging each other, donning the purple robes, chanting mantras and playing little tunes on their finger cymbals.

We had such a good time that I decided there and then to take the Dalai out again. I wasn't going to let the Chinese or anyone else stop me. I met the Dalai later in the week in Sydney and took him to the State of Origin at Telstra Stadium.

Bill Harrigan knows the path to true enlightenment can be found directly up his left nostril

Now, the Dalai Lama wears the maroon colours but the truth is he was barracking for a draw. I'd tried to explain to him about the golden goal and extra-time rules but he wouldn't have a bar of it. He thought a draw was the only way all the players would find inner peace.

So I realised the Dalai was onto something there. Besides, the bookies were offering astronomical odds on the draw, so I put a few bob on it. I thought, you never know, the Dalai Lama moves in mysterious ways.

That's because he's got the third eye working for him. The third eye or ajna chakra is the gateway to all transcendental or metaphysical states of consciousness. The Dalai Lama's third eye allows him to see the winners of a horserace before they jump and he could make a truckload of money out of it but that sort of thing isn't really his go.

Think of it like a video referee in the grandstand of life. The third eye or video referee sees all and can correct any mistakes we might make along the way – but only if we are so enlightened as to listen. If you're enlightened, it can be like having Bill Harrigan sitting on your shoulder throughout the life cycle, telling you if you're onside or not.

It'd be a very handy thing to have but my third eye often appears to be on the blink.

Still, it must have been fully functional at the State of Origin. I'd had a dabble on the draw with the Dalai Lama but I'd thrown some big money on the Maroons to win. Queensland came away with the points and I won a motser. The Dalai Lama didn't seem to mind that he'd done his dough. I think he was just grateful that there was someone in Australia who would go out of their way to show him a good time.

The Hillsong Happy Clappers

Name	Hillsong Church
Deity	Mammon
Leader	One of the twenty interchangeable cyborgs known as Pastor Brian Houston
Holy Book	*Jesus Wants Poor People To Kill Themselves*
Can you get a drink?	Yes, but from a $45 novelty thermos with a winking Jesus on it.
Can you get a root?	Yes, but it'll come out in the papers eventually. That's when you must command Satan to get out of your genitals. In public.

These gargoyles with fake tans scare the shit out of me. I mean, look at them.

The man with piano keys for teeth is Brian Houston, the pastor of Hillsong. Some years ago Brian wrote a tremendous book called *You Need More Money*. Quite frankly, I found the title to be deeply inspirational.

Then I saw the subtitle, *Discovering God's Amazing Financial Plan for Your Life*, and I became a bit suss. The last time someone came on to me with an unsolicited financial plan, I bought a large pile of bat guano some six thousand feet underwater off the coast of Nauru.

But I had a quick flick through the book and I read that 'anyone who puts the Kingdom of God first can expect bible economics to work in their life NOW'. So after I pinched it off the shelf from the Hillsong gift shoppe, I was off to a good start.

Every Sunday the Hillsongers put on a service in a stadium somewhere in outer Sydney for five hundred thousand hysterical Christians in the throes of religious ecstasy. They must be doing something right because John Howard, Peter Costello and Bob Carr have shown up and strummed guitars and generally pretended they were having the time of their lives.

God's amazing financial plan has come true for Brian in any case. Brian owns a Harley-Davidson hog, a Breitling watch and acres of Country Road black skivvies.

After Brian got the Harley, he called me over and wanted to know what I thought. I told him he looked as hardcore as Donny Osmond in his 'Soldier of Love' period. I said, 'Brian, it wouldn't matter if you got a Prince Albert and dangled lumps of coal from your swingers: you'd still look like a Christian. And if you ever call me "dude" again, I'll kill you.'

Brian Houston: radical orofacial surgery has helped but the pastor still endures the pain of 'Grinner's Palsy' – a rare disorder that has snapped his face in a permanent idiotic grin

The Scientologists

Name	Scientology
Deity	You need to spend $40,000 before you get to find that out, my friend.
Leader	The frozen corpse of L. Ron Hubbard
Holy Book	*Battlefield Earth*
Can you get a drink?	Would you like to do a free personality test?
Can you get a root?	Would you like to do a free personality test?

This crowd seriously weird me out. Some years ago little Katie Ceberano asked me to play banjo for her band on a tour of the US. Before I could join the group I had to be strapped to something called an 'E-meter' and undergo a free personality test with 40,000 volts travelling through my genitals. I agreed at once out of curiosity. The test revealed I had all sorts of personal problems that I had been unaware of. By the end of it I was a sobbing mess and I had to neck six schooners of Mandarine Napoléon just to calm down.

When we got to LA, Katie put me up in one of their 'Celebrity Centers'. This is like a five-star hotel, except the sheilas who join you in the jacuzzi won't crack on to you unless you agree to read some science fiction.

So I agreed to read some of L. Ron Hubbard's theories of the origin of the universe. Apparently it all goes back to an alien called Xenu who was the dictator of the 'Galactic Confederacy'. Around 75 million years ago, Xenu brought billions of aliens to Earth in a spaceship that looked a lot like an old DC-8, then stacked them around volcanoes and blew them up with hydrogen bombs. Their souls clustered together and stuck to the bodies of the living, and continue to wreak chaos and havoc today. When you see it put that way, it makes a lot of sense.

Xenu: supreme dictator of the Galactic Confederacy. It's all his fault.

Today we have much to thank Scientology for. Without the glorious theories of L. Ron Hubbard we wouldn't have *Battlefield Earth*, the E-meter or the impenetrable confidence of Tom Cruise.

In Australia Scientology is recognised as a church, but in Germany the authorities see it as a dangerous totalitarian cult, which, quite frankly, is an interesting assessment coming from that mob.

In America Scientologists have been accused of infiltrating the highest levels of government to get favourable decisions from them. Thank Christ, that could never happen here.

The Exclusive Brethren

A weird little cult if ever there was one. Members of the Exclusive Brethren are prohibited from voting but apparently this doesn't constrain them from telling others how to go about it.

They dress their women in clothes that the Amish would find prudish and routinely exile cult members for the heinous crime of watching television.

The leader of this happy bunch of campers is known as the Elect Vessel which means he is full of the elixir of life and plans to spray plenty of it about during long private prayer sessions with the womenfolk.

They would be the most appalling human beings to ever cast a shadow on the planet if it wasn't for the fact that they hate the Greens even more than I do.

Name	Exclusive Brethren
Deity	God in a shirt buttoned up to the neck and in a pair of crimplene trousers.
Leader	The Elect Vessel
Holy Book	The Bible (with the naughty bits deleted)
Can you get a drink?	Definitely not. What do you think this is, Gomorrah?
Can you get a root?	That's not a television I can hear in the background, is it?

The Exclusive Brethren's leader in the 1960s, 'Big Jim' Taylor, combined his work with the brethren with several solid performances at full-back for West Torrens in the SANFL

The Mormons

Name	Mormonism
Deity	A god, almost identical to the Christian God, but with thicker hair and a beard like Santa.
Leader	Gordon B. Hinckley, the biggest Mormon in the whole, wide world
Holy Book	Whatever happened to those golden plates, anyway?
Can you get a drink?	No, but would you like a glass of unfluoridated water or decocoanated cocoa?
Can you get a root?	You've got a different wife for every day of the week, so in practical terms, no.

I have become much more kindly disposed to these people since they stopped calling on me on a Sunday morning. Mistakes were made on both sides but I deny the charges and I still don't believe that the police should have been summoned. The matter is with the courts now and I can say little more other than it was unpleasant for all concerned.

Mormons believe that a nineteenth-century con man was Jesus Christ reincarnated and that Native Americans are Jews. They don't drink coffee or tea or take any drugs, not even for recreational purposes. They fuck like rabbits and marry their cousins, often many times over.

They may not let drugs or alcohol pass their lips but whatever it is they are taking, put me down for half-a-dozen right now.

Mormon leader Gordon B. Hinckley waves to one of his thirty-seven wives, during his thirtieth birthday bash

The Hare Krishnas

No doubt you've encountered these cheerful creatures in a pedestrian mall, hopping about, pounding a drum, chinging their finger cymbals on a Sunday morning – when you've got a force ten hangover.

The Krishnas believe that your soul has fallen from the spiritual world to this material world and that the whole point of your crappy little life is to become Krishna-conscious and return to Godhead.

This is achieved by repeating a simple mantra over and over again, much the same way the treasurer bangs on about the childcare rebate.

The Krishnas play at being hippie flowerchildren but the truth is, they're more repressive than the Catholic Church. No sex, no drugs, no beer, no coffee. That's just the start of it. No surf'n'turf, no Happy Meals, no pie nights, no cigs, no orgiastic transgender frenzies. No crack cocaine. Not even an ecstasy enema.

So what do these painted bedsheet wearers do for a giggle? How about a finger cymbal concert, a vegetable pakora and three days of farting?

Name	Hare Krishna
Deity	Krishna, an avatar of Vishnu – a god with four arms who can have a beer, a smoke, read the form guide and get one off the wrist at the same time.
Leader	Bhaktivedanta Swami Prabhupadabahagatajkanam-aoapalahahajahafacabanama-hagataramhafgakanahayatag-abanakalananagamama. He shares his name with a small Welsh village.
Holy Book	The *Bhagavad Gita*: a discourse on the ideals of universal harmony and duty. You should force your kids to read it.
Can you get a drink?	No. Or a steak. Or a chop. A suckling pig on a spit is completely out of the question.
Can you get a root?	In theory no. But most of the followers are hippie chicks, so, yes.

Swami Thingo: he's got it all sussed out

The Jains

Name	Jainism
Deity	The unchanging traits of the pure soul of each living being, whatever that means.
Leader	They haven't had a damned good leader since Manahvir Swami, who turned his toes up in 527BC, but that doesn't mean they're not looking for one.
Holy Book	*Entymology for Beginners*
Can you get a drink?	Only if you don't want one. It's a very strange religion.
Can you get a root?	Yes but for the love of God make sure you don't crush any dust mites while you're doing it.

Jainism is a wonderful religion, replete with some very fine ideals. Jainism accounts for .04 per cent of the world's religious followers, so you know they won't take just anybody. Unlike the Catholics and Anglicans, you've got to do a bit more than just turn up on a Sunday and sing a song or two to get a guernsey with the Jains.

There are five basic tenets to Jainism – nonviolence, truth, respect for others' property, chastity and open-mindedness. Of course any reasonable Australian will have defenestrated each and every one of these in the space of three hours on the drink.

Jainism kicked off about two-and-a-half thousand years ago and has gone gangbusters ever since.

Jains wear masks to spare the lives of tiny insects that may pop into their gobs at any given moment. And that's why the religion has never really established a solid base in Australia. In Australia there are simply too many flying critters hurling themselves about the place. It's only a matter of time before one zooms through the gaps in your teeth and heads straight down your alimentary canal to die horribly in a pool of digestive acid.

Jainism had a bit of a following here early on but the Great Blowfly Massacre of 1968, when a Jain swallowed fifteen blowflies in one careless breath after falling in a vat of manure in Dapto, put paid to that.

He was excommunicated – received a very nice letter politely asking him to move along quietly, without killing any more bugs. Or else he'd receive another nice letter and another and so on.

That's the fundamental problem with your Jain. He just doesn't get angry. A Jain won't back you up in a blue. If you're on the piss in a nightclub with some Jains and you get into a spot of bother, you have to understand right off the bat, you're on your own.

In Jainism, fat people are carried around in chairs to prevent the tragedy of pratfall-related insect crushings

Zoroastrianism

Name	Zoroastrianism
Deity	Ahura Mazda
Leader	I don't know. It's a very small religion. I can't be expected to know everything.
Holy Book	*The Gathas*. I'm told it's a bestseller in Indian airports.
Can you get a drink?	I don't know. Can't you find this out for yourself? Fuck's sake
Can you get a root?	Look, I've had a gutful of this. Let's just move on.

The only cult worth a candle, in my book. Zoroastrianism was conceived in Persia a couple of thousand years ago. It's never really taken off in Australia but it could be the religion to watch when the Hillsong kiddies finally realise they've been swindled.

The Zoroastrian god is named after a Japanese car and the central theme of the religion is making sure when loved ones die they get a decent send-off. So when a spouse dies, the corpse is slung out onto the roof, where the gang-gang cockatoos and Indian mynahs help themselves to a top feed, starting with the eyeballs. In a couple of days' time, the cadaver is gone, sitting in the bellies of birds. It's an air burial, or at least the Zoroastrians seem to think so.

The fact that the loved one comes back to Earth to rest on statues of fallen soldiers and great Australian heroes is something that has never occurred to them.

Still, I think they're on to something, so I put my mum out on the roof. She climbed back in through the manhole a few minutes later and was none too pleased. There's just no helping some people.

Zoroastrianists at play: a night out with some crap fireworks and they're as happy as pigs in shit

Rock Botherers

Rock botherers or animists are generally of the dusky-hued persuasion and haven't got the television on yet. They believe that gods live in trees and rocks and sometimes underground. They spend most of their time bowing and scraping to rocks and sacrificing pigs and young sheilas to keep the rocks happy.

It's not a bad sort of life and some of their rituals can be quite enjoyable provided that it's not you strapped to the sacrificial altar with an apple in your mouth.

Name	Animism
Deity	Too numerous to mention
Leader	The guy with the biggest penis gourd
Holy Book	A hand print spray-painted on a rock that in many ways says so much but in others says too little.
Can you get a drink?	Sure. Try the virgin's blood and lion semen combo. Be careful, it's got a kick to it.
Can you get a root?	Knock yourself out, just keep your filthy fucking hands off my goat.

This might look like just a rock to you but to animists it's the fucking Sistine Chapel

The Cult of Bindi Irwin

Name	Bindiism
Deity	Steve Irwin
Leader	Duh!
Holy Book	*The Crocodile Hunter* (two-volume set on DVD)
Can you get a drink?	Why not purchase one at the gift shop?
Can you get a root?	You might want to check with the gift shop on that.

Reptile management is right up there with healing cripples and bread distribution at large public gatherings as a sign of other-worldly powers. Little Bindi Irwin is seen by cult members to have inherited all the powers of her late father and she's thrown in a certain perkiness of her own. Such is her charisma, she's now followed everywhere by a group of apostles called 'Croc Men', who study her every movement and turn it into jazz ballet.

She's a terrific young lass and completely deserves to be venerated as a pagan goddess of reptile theme parks.

Bindi and her mum keeping the kiddies happy. It's her adult followers who are of greater concern.

The Atheists

You can stop sounding superior, you're going to hell.

Name	Atheism
Deity	Mindless consumerism
Leader	Christopher Hitchens Richard Dawkins
Holy Book	*God is Not Great* *The God Delusion* *Color Climax No. 146*
Can you get a drink?	As many or as few as you like. It doesn't matter. You're going to hell.
Can you get a root?	Go for your life. Root your arse off. Let's see what your libido makes of the sulphurous fumes of Hades.

Hell, yesterday

The Secret of the Universe

I've tried every religion there is and the truth is, they've all got it wrong. Dead wrong. Now that you've got this far, I may as well tell you how the universe and afterlife really work, so you won't go wasting your hard-earned on silly hats and frankincense.

First off: the Buddhists, the Muslims, the Hindus are miles away. Those scary little Christian evangelicals? Not even close. I know this for a fact. I was privileged to be given a glimpse of the shape of the universe first hand.

Some years ago I accompanied some Cabinet ministers on a root and snort tour of Tibet, courtesy of the Chinese Government. One night in Lhasa, the boys and I were in a ladyboy strip club. (Ladyboys are almost impossible to find in Tibet, but after some loud complaining from our party, the Chinese obligingly flew in a dozen from Bangkok that morning. The Chinese are terrific hosts.)

Anyway, that night one of these bewitching creatures slipped me a drink. It was a concoction of magic mushrooms, hashish and fermented goat's blood, all whizzed up in a Bamix, with a sprinkle of nutmeg on top.

I reckon it was the nutmeg that did me in.

The effect of this drink was to free me from the moorings of time and space, to let me stand outside our universe and apprehend it as a whole. What I saw shocked me to the core.

It turns out that our universe, the whole box and dice, everything we know and hold dear, exists inside a tiny bubble of air inside a massive KitKat bar that sits inside the sock drawer of a giant called Big Roger.

Big Roger has lost the KitKat bar; he's forgotten he even bought it. But when he finds it, we're fucked. The bloke is notorious on the nosebag, spends a lot of time on the couch and has regular cravings for chocolate treats that may or may not contain traces of nuts.

When the penny drops, that's it my friend. Bend over and kiss your arse goodbye. That's all there is to it. Armageddon outta here. So you can drop all the complex rules and commandments. There's only one rule that makes any sense: Don't draw attention to the KitKat. And keep your voice down, for Christ's sake.

Big Roger: you live in his KitKat

CHAPTER TEN

Elections

Australia Tosses a Coin

It's All About the Result

On election night I'm there at the National Tally Room. I'm the bloke at the back of the board turning over the numbers as the results come in. It's a terrific job: the Australian Electoral Commission always puts on a topnotch feed and they employ a couple of kids to hand me schooners of anisette throughout the night. Number turning is thirsty work, I can tell you. It's a huge responsibility.

I'm generally considered to be one of the top number-turners in the number-turning business. I do a bit of this sort of work – strictly on a voluntary basis, just in case the taxman is reading this.

I've been turning numbers at the tally room at every election since 1974. Since you've done the right thing and forked out a few bucks of your hard-earned for this book, I feel I should let you in on a big secret: Snedden actually won the 1974 election. But the man was a train wreck waiting to happen, so I fiddled around, turned a few 6's into 9's and Gough was back for another term. The big man was very grateful to me and he made sure there was always a big drink around the traps for me in the ensuing years.

Election night 2004, the National Tally Room: that's me at the back in the cardigan

In 2004, Latham won by a landslide but I knew he was clinically insane and would put the country in a spiral of self loathing. Cab drivers across the nation wouldn't be safe for a start, so I bunged on a few thousand votes in the right places and little Johnnie Winston made his acceptance speech that night.

Howard said he was humbled by the win and, let's face it, he's not a man given to humility under normal circumstances. I can tell you now he was humbled only because he knew he lost by the numbers and he owed me a very large debt of gratitude.

No-one ever seems to notice or mind and I like to think I am just reflecting the broad views of the nation. I understand that people can get confused at the ballot box and I've always been happy to straighten out any unintended voting behaviour.

This job gives me a unique perspective on the way our system works. And I can confidently say that Australia has the best electoral system in the world, bar none. But we can always improve things. Near enough is good enough has never been good enough for me. We never would have got the cardboard voting booth with that kind of thinking.

Allow me to share a few sensible proposals for electoral reform with you.

Winning

Nothing disgusts the ordinary voter so much as watching the winner claim victory on television. They see a man they can barely tolerate beaming with a pleasure so intense that it's creepily sexual (which is why they always put a podium in front of him so the voters won't notice the rampant Shirvington pants action down below).

And worst of all, they see the winner in a room full of people on the piss, having a party that they haven't been invited to. No wonder ordinary Australians are so disaffected.

That's why I say there ought to be some sort of legal requirement for the winner to shout a drink for every man, woman and child in the nation. Out of their own pocket. This would do much to create goodwill with the public and encourage citizens to overlook the winner's huge reserves of megalomania and hatred.

Losing

The biggest problem is making politicians more responsive to the will of the people outside of the three-week election campaign. The answer is quite simple and it came to me in a blinding flash of inspiration as I lay under a bar in Thailand after a three-day drinking excursion with the Australian Cricket Team. Are you ready for this? Here it is: *Losing an election should be illegal.*

The party that loses the election has been found wanting by the Australian people and should consequently be made to pay for their sins. The prospect of a stint in jail would do wonders for politicians' commitment to the voters. It would raise the stakes enormously and make the leaders' debate much more interesting.

To make losing an offence punishable by a stretch of fifteen to twenty years in the slammer, bunking in with good, wholesome heterosexual folk who, as circumstances dictate, are prepared to experiment sexually, would be an enormous performance incentive. Most experts agree it would go a long way to reconnecting the parties with ordinary punters.

If I had my way, right now Mark Latham would be in the clink, along with John Hewson and Keating. Little Johnnie Howard would only now be walking out of the prison gates for having lost the 1987 election and we would have been spared the last decade of arse covering and shoulder twitching.

It's such an obviously sensible proposal; it's beyond me why it hasn't been taken up thus far.

How to Win an Election

Every couple of years a government gets itself into deep shit and that's when I get the call to come and help. My advice to the hapless leader is always the same:

- **Ditch the focus groups**
  Most politicians lead deeply weird and insular lives and are completely reliant on focus group reports to acquaint themselves with what's going on in the real world. But the results are unreliable. Focus groups are made up of ordinary people, which means they're greedy bastards who'll tell a whole pack of lies to look good. They'll put their hand up and say they're concerned about global warming, education and sustainability, but the truth is they'll kick a field full of pandas to death in order to get to a tax cut. So I tell them: forget the focus groups; instead . . .

- **Go with the gut instinct**
  I always go with my gut instinct, even when that instinct has led me to a Chinese meal which left me crouching in agony in the ensuite. Politically speaking, your gut is your best friend. Forget the Jiminy Cricket of conscience on your shoulder; you're better off listening to the python of self-interest slowly uncoiling in your stomach.

- **Be a scumbag for a day**
  I always remind the leader that the great Roman emperor, Augustus Caesar, didn't need any market research to find out what the mob wanted. Every year, for one day, the crafty bugger would disguise himself as a beggar and sit on the streets of Rome, drinking schooners of grappa, listening to what the punters had to say, and that was all he needed. So I tell the leader: smear yourself with human faeces, go to a railway tunnel and try busking some Neil Young songs. You'll quickly discover that a spirited rendition of 'Heart of Gold' will earn you more coins than a dozen performances of 'The Needle and the Damage Done'. Find out what the people want.

- **Walk a mile in my shoes**
  I invite the embattled leader to come and live with me for a week. I make up a bed in the granny flat out the back and order the gormless clown to follow me everywhere and get a sense of what my real-world issues are.

  Like why is it that toilet paper never tears properly on the dotted line?

  And how come ABC Sport only rarely covers the lawn bowls these days? And where the fuck can a bloke go to get a drink and watch harness racing at 10 am on a Good Friday?

  And why do I always have to ask the yum cha waiter to bring me some chilli sauce and an ouzo and coke? Why can't they just have it on the table with the soy sauce and the chopsticks?

  These are the issues that connect with ordinary Australians. Who gives two shits about the current account deficit when you've got this crap to deal with on a daily basis?

ALL THOSE IN FAVOUR

Nowadays on election day you front up at a primary school and then struggle through your contesting feelings of hatred for each of the candidates on the paper in front of you. It's a farce and everyone knows it. But it wasn't always like this. Back in the fifties, Bob Menzies would simply appear on the steps of Parliament House at 3 am on a cold Canberra morning and quietly ask anyone present whether his government should be returned. It was decided on the voices, saving all the needless expense and acrimony of dragging the country out of bed on a Saturday morning.

Great Election Nights in Australian History
A Personal Scrapbook

2 December 1972: It's Time – for a very big drink

The election that ends twenty-three years of Coalition rule. New prime minister Gough Whitlam arrives in triumph at the tally room, but is quickly assailed by ALP loyalists seeking government employment.

18 May 1974: Gough accepts victory in the company of a couple of Treasury officials

Gough scrapes back in. Opposition leader Billy Snedden concedes defeat by saying, 'We didn't win, but we didn't lose either.' An entire Tibetan monastery is still studying the implications of this fascinating paradox.

13 December 1975: Gougherdämmerung

Labor gets clobbered. Gough is so stunned by the scale of his defeat, he fails to regain his senses until late 1977, when doctors regretfully have to inform him that he's lost another election by an even bigger margin. The new PM is Malcolm Fraser, who has campaigned on the slogan, 'Turn On the Lights'. On this night Fraser is still blissfully unaware that other things will be required of him beyond merely flicking on light switches, such as managing an economy.

5 March 1983: Hawke successfully elected on a platform to 'Destroy Puny Humans'

Malcolm Fraser goes down with a pitiless thud. In his concession speech he claims he's leaving the country in good shape, which leaves even his staffers coughing the word 'bullshit' under their breath. Bob Hawke shows up at the tally room with his wife and is cheered to the rafters. At this moment of triumph, Hawke reveals he is in fact a bug-eyed alien and that he will 'crush the puny humans'. This is ignored. But revelations that he has given up the grog are greeted with deep disquiet by a worried electorate.

11 July 1987: Hawke beats Howard

Even though the economy is as sour as a fish milkshake, Hawkie increases his majority – mainly because the electorate just isn't ready to go take a flying leap into the past with John Howard. Oddly enough, that moment still lies in the future. Howard concedes defeat graciously with the statesman-like utterance: 'The things that unite us are much more important than the things that divide us.' A decade later Howard becomes the most divisive prime minister since Billy Hughes. Just looking at this pic (with the word 'again' in the background), I'm overcome by a sense of deep weariness at the number of times I've had to look at this joyless, ugly mug on an election night. This bloke could walk into a room full of drunks and have them all stone-cold sober and worried about their superannuation in twenty minutes.

13 March 1993: Keating wins and John Hewson's meteoric career hits a glitch

Looking at this pic gets me all emotional. There he is: he's got the prime ministership. He's still got his missus. And he's still got his hands on the levers of power. These days all he's got his hands on is a second-hand furniture catalogue.

The Keating Government is returned, despite having led the nation into the worst recession in sixty years. The Opposition leader comes a cropper in the campaign where the central galvanising issue is the cost of birthday cakes. Keating claims victory for the 'true believers' – and if you believed he'd deliver on those 'L-A-W' tax cuts then you'd believe anything. Keating governs for the next three years under the mistaken impression that everyone in Australia lives in Darlinghurst. John Hewson makes a disgrace of himself during the campaign by telling the truth about his intentions for Australia. The electorate rightly pings him for his impertinence. Truth-telling in an election is like farting in the cathedral: it's honest, but it lacks decorum. Fortunately no party has repeated that mistake since 1993.

2 March 1996: The old gelding finally salutes at the leger

There he is. Howard has successfully nagged the nation into electing him. Maybe now, he figures, his missus will stop calling him a complete failure.

Keating concedes defeat and wanders off into the sunset. The following day he hits the phones and finds job for all of his staff, forgetting to find one for himself.

3 October 1998: Bomber crashes, declares diet 'officially over'

Kim Beazley comes in ahead on the two-party preferred vote, but Howard beats him on the vote spread and is re-elected. Beazley makes such a good impression with his warm, good-hearted concession speech that voters conclude they'd like to see him make another one just like it three years later. Later in the night, Big Kim breaks his campaign diet by attempting to consume his upper lip, causing great distress to his family and staff.

10 November 2001: Learn-to-swim carnival fails to distract voters, Howard shits it in

With a 3 per cent swing the Howard Government is re-elected with an increased majority in the Lower House and Kim Beazley is consigned to the dustbin of history. As New York City smoulders after the 9/11 terrorist attack and the world is in turmoil, voters very sensibly determine that this is no time to have Kim Beazley's vast frame sticking out of the turret of an M1 Abrams tank.

The Australian Electoral Commission is roundly criticised for creating floating polling booths in the Indian Ocean. Many voters turn up only to discover that their votes are invalid. Happily, they were all sent on a trip to the South Pacific as compensation.

9 October 2004: Mark Latham implodes, leaving a sticky mess all over the Labor Party

Latham loses after the voters make a glib, unfair character judgement based entirely on a single handshake. Their judgement turns out to be entirely correct. Mark Latham resigns and returns to his favourite pastime: punching out people in the service industries.

The results give John Howard control of the Senate. For the umpteenth time he says he's 'humbled' by his victory. It's a lay-down misère that when he loses, he'll say he's 'proud' of his government's achievements.

CHAPTER ELEVEN

Make Your Mark

Come On In

You're Just About Done

So do you get it now? You better have. I'm not going through that again, I can tell you now. If you've been listening (and personally I have my doubts) you will now have an explicit understanding of how Australia works and how to pick the plum from the tree and help yourself to its succulent appetisingness.

I've knocked together a bit of a do-it-yourself guide, like the ones you get at Bunnings when you're knocking together a bit of a play house for the kiddies. But this is far more important. This contains important information on how to make your mark in Australia: how to dress, what to drink, where to go, who to knock around with. If you can get these right, you're well on your way.

Stand Inside the Tent Pissing Out

The first thing you need to get is some mates. And to get mates, you need to join a club. Some of them will get you where you need to go. Other clubs are full of low-grade bottom-feeding shits who still can't find it in their hearts to forgive a few minor transgressions which happened fuckin' years ago.

Collingwood Football Club

Lots of fun, but it doesn't really get you anywhere except much closer to Eddie McGuire than you'd ever really want to be. Becoming a member is an awkward and embarrassing business. First you need to track down and kill someone from Carlton, then burn his house to the ground and the orphanage that his children were sent to. Thank Christ I'll never have to go through that again.

Then you're brought in front of the portrait of Jock McHale and made to drop your strides while the entire board inspects your manhood and makes disparaging remarks. I never minded that part and just brushed it off as high-spirited hazing. Then they tie a black and white ribbon around your genitals and you're sent back to your girlfriend. So don't do it unless you really, really have to.

And if you've ever been a member of another team's club, you need to get that membership formally annulled by the Pope. It's all too hard.

The Hellfire Club

Hugely overrated. It's true that very successful people often populate these evenings. But a rich dickhead in a gimp suit is still just a dickhead in a gimp suit. In this day and age, when even your local newsagent has a leather corset and a pierced nipple, perhaps it's time to try something a bit different.

The Melbourne Club

Not what it used to be. In its heyday it was a haven for the idiot sons of Victoria's squattocracy; a place where they felt free to savour the heady pleasures of anti-Semitic humour and sheep dip recipes. Those days are long gone but the Melbourne Club is still a good place to gain entree into the Liberal Party. The downside is you have to hang out with Liberals.

The Freemasons

It used to be compulsory to be a mason if you wanted any sort of career in the Treasury Department or in any of the police forces. Unfortunately the whole tone of the place has dropped since they admitted Catholics. But the rituals are hugely entertaining and I give them an extra star for that.

The Freemasons were invented as a way for blokes to get away from their wives and put on an apron. No, I've never been able to figure that one out either.

They worship a triple-headed deity called 'Jahbulon', a mix-up of Yahweh the god of the Hebrews, Baal the god of the Canaanites and Osiris from the Egyptians, and I say good luck to them. They call God 'The Great Architect', but the last time I employed an architect with three heads I was coming down after an AMT and Midori cocktail. The bastard built me a block of flats with no stairs, windows or doorways.

The American Club

This joint has a very swish clubhouse and becoming a member affords you the opportunity of getting on the piss occasionally with Dick Cheney and telling him exactly what you think of him. Watch out you don't accidentally get conscripted to fight and die in some Middle Eastern shithole.

Rooty Hill RSL

A tremendous place; more like a resort than a club. Where else could you help yourself to a huge roast from a bain-marie, drink beer on tap, watch Daryl Braithwaite belt out 'Howzat' from the stage and then dance the night away to a Pink Floyd tribute band? Nowhere, that's where.

The Cat Protection Society

The best of the lot. On the surface, the CPS is a shopfront of old biddies who spend all day stroking moggies and slowly drinking themselves to death with sweet sherry. Don't be fooled; this is just a smokescreen to disguise an elite cadre of highly skilled, ruthless operators, silently shifting the furniture of reality.

It's Your Shout: Thinking and Drinking in Australia

Pick the ideology that best represents your conscience and your preferred alcoholic beverage. Clip these out and present them at the appropriate party's biennial conference to receive a complimentary drink at the hotel bar.

GREEN/LEFT
Party: **The Greens**
Beverage of choice:
Well, that depends. First you have to ask: was it made by exploited workers? Were any animals harmed in the production of the . . .

SOCIAL DEMOCRAT
Party: **The ALP**
Beverage of choice:
Sauvignon Blanc (Chardonnay is so, like, everywhere these days)

CENTRIST
Party:
The Australian Democrats
Beverage of choice:
Hard, hard liquor

CONSERVATIVE
Party: **The Liberals**
Beverage of choice:
Grange Hermitage (Tooheys New when in front of the voters)

CHRISTIAN DEMOCRAT
Party: **Family First**
Beverage of choice: Cod-liver oil and the heady ambrosia of self-righteousness

REACTIONARY
Party: **One Nation**
Beverage of choice:
The bitter dregs of hatred left to us by the hordes of immigrants who have taken our jobs

NON-ALIGNED: Not everyone sits inside this neat little spectrum, my friend. There are other groups you might want to consider . . .

ISLAMO-FASCIST
Party: **al-Qaeda**
Beverage of choice:
The wine-dark blood of the infidel

FEMINAZI
Party: **I'm above all that now.**
Beverage of choice:
Breast milk and carob milkshakes

AGRARIAN SOCIALIST
Party: **Nationals**
Beverage of choice:
We've had nowt to drink for nigh on five years now . . .

Jobs for the Boys: Picking the Right Drinks Trolley

You've put in the hard yards. You had the foresight to drop a brown paper bag to an Opposition leader back when everyone thought a psoriatic orangutan stood a better chance of getting elected. Now your man's in government and he's deeply grateful. The gravy train is leaving the station and you're sitting up the front. But don't be a mug. Don't rush in and take just any old appointment. It's time to unfold the map of the world and go for the gig with the best drinks trolley. Consult this chart before you even think of returning that phone call.

JOB	SCHOONER RATING	PROS	CONS	OTHER CONTENDERS
High Commissioner to London		The sweetest nut. No-one knows you're there or what you're supposed to be doing, so you can help yourself to everything.	Having to fight off ERII after she's had a few shandies. Old Liz is good for a laugh but she's a bugger on the piss.	Any current financial member of the Liberal Party
Ambassador to Ireland and the Holy See		Sign a few documents in the morning and then get as drunk as an Irishman all day long.	Long, boring masses. You can't smoke in front of the Pope.	Kim Beazley Wilson Tuckey
Ambassador to the United States		Big breakfasts, long lunches. You're shit-faced by dinner time.	Americans presume you're from Austria and speak loudly to you if they ever speak to you at all.	Bob Carr Teresa Gambaro
Chief Justice of the High Court		Make whatever laws you want and throw out any you don't like.	A lot of sitting down.	Phillip Ruddock Hotman Paris Hutapea
Consul-General in Los Angeles		You are constantly seen in the company of Hollywood celebrities.	You are constantly in the company of Hollywood celebrities.	Malcolm Turnbull Julia Gillard
Ambassador to the United Nations		An all-expenses-paid apartment on the Upper West Side of Manhattan.	Too many foreigners.	Kevin Rudd Alexander Downer
Governor-General		Nice house. Servants. As many kangaroos as you can eat. That prick of a PM has to call you 'Your Excellency'.	You have to wear a hat.	Shane Warne The crippled kiddie on *A Current Affair*

DAME PATTIE MENZIES AND THE ORIGIN OF THE SCHOONER

The original champagne glass is said to have been moulded from the breast of Marie Antoinette. Likewise, the Australian schooner glass is thought to be moulded from the left funbag of Dame Pattie Menzies; the perfect shape for consuming vast amounts of beer in such a way that you never get tired of it.

JOB	SCHOONER RATING	PROS	CONS	OTHER CONTENDERS
Director, Australian Wheat Board		Limitless expense account, guns and ammo.	Jail.	John Anderson John Bjelke-Petersen
Chairman of the ABC		Lots of telly.	Most of it shithouse.	John Burgess Naomi Robson
Human Rights and Equal Opportunity Commissioner		You become the moral heart of the country.	You have to stop looking at pornography at work.	Pru Goward Germaine Greer
Director, Telstra		Insider trading opportunities everywhere you look.	At board meetings, you're made to sit in the corner and think about what you did.	Jeff Kennett Andrew Peacock
Chief Scientist		Write your own prescriptions. If all goes well your face could end up on a $500 note one day.	Part-time position. You have to be good at maths.	Ian Campbell Barry Jones
High Commissioner to Papua New Guinea		None.	The High Commission in Port Moresby is looted every Wednesday at 3 o'clock sharp.	Barnaby Joyce Bill Shorten

Philip Ruddock: Dead or Alive – Who Knows?

If you're ever called to a meeting with Philip Ruddock, one of the first things you must figure out is whether he's alive or dead on that particular day.

Ruddock with the media: close observation reveals flecks of embalming fluid in the hair. Probably dead here.

Once I fell into conversation with Philip Ruddock at a function and mistakenly thought the man was alive. I assumed from his rigor mortis smile that he was merely fascinated by my thoughts on the parlous state of harness racing in this country, but it turns out the bugger was brown bread all along. It was hugely embarrassing for all concerned.

Some months later I saw him again at a fundraiser and I wasn't sure if he was still dead, so I poked him with a stick. By then he was attorney-general and so he sicked the federal police on me. That cost me more than a few cartons of duty-free cigs, I can tell you.

Even though members of Ruddock's own family recoil in horror at his presence, I've always admired his work as immigration minister in the golden years of the Howard Government. Ruddock was perfect for the job; the kind of bloke who would never take any shit from the wrongfully imprisoned.

When the tired, the poor, the huddled masses washed up on our shores yearning to breathe free, Ruddock held up a megaphone and told them to pull off a ticket from the deli counter or fuck off back home.

Ruddock got the job at immigration because he was the only man who could make mandatory detention of traumatised children sound like a good idea.

The nay-sayers said it wasn't possible, but he got the job done. And if he hadn't, today we'd have literally thousands of young kiddies haunting Australia's playgrounds, frightening the hell out of the others with their tales of genocide, torture, and what it's like to live in a country where the nearest Happy Meal is more than fourteen hours' drive away.

Philip Ruddock, flogging used cars: if he isn't dead here, he should be

In 2005 Ruddock suddenly dropped dead in the House and banged into the prime minister. He was reanimated afterwards by an injection of human growth hormone and chicken semen.

Anyway, before you meet up with Ruddock, cut out this checklist and observe him for these vital signs of incipient dead-ness:

1. *Ignore his complexion.* People make this judgement call all the time. It's a big mistake because 'pale and waxy' is Ruddock's default mode, dead and alive. Instead . . .

2. *Check his breath.* If it's foul and rancid, don't assume it's a sign of putrefaction; it's probably due to the infants' blood he gargles each morning. If he's breathing then he's definitely alive (on that day at least).

3. *Is the bastard smiling?* If he's smiling like a drag queen after a Botox injection, he's probably dead.

4. *Listen to what he says.* See if he uses his stock phrase 'in relation to . . .' more than twenty times a minute. If so, that means his staff have inserted a tape loop inside his coit again and he's definitely dead. I've seen him skip through several *7.30 Report* interviews with this technique.

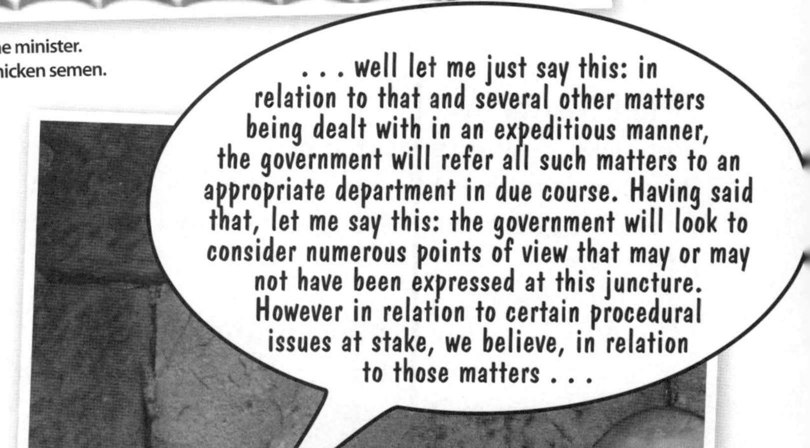

Philip Ruddock answers questions about the weather

What to Wear to a Long Lunch with . . .

The Premier

Premiers tend to wear the same outfit every single day, even on weekends, on the off-chance they'll get the call from Barrie Cassidy to go on *Insiders* to speak about regional irrigation.

Whatever the premier's favourite outfit is, you should wear exactly the same thing. A premier is a chippy bastard; although he dominates his state, odds are he bitterly wishes that he'd gone federal. The thought that he might have had a crack at the prime ministership gnaws at his soul every single night.

So don't try and smart-arse these characters: complete and total agreement with every comment they make, no matter how stupid and dangerous, is the way to go. *Yes Premier, I too think your Cabinet rival is a lying c— with a limited future.*

The PM's Wife

You need a bit of street cred here. The PM's wife deals with boring suits all day long so try something different. It's a little-known fact that the first lady has a thing for gangsta rap. So dress like ghetto trash. Bling it up. Show the 'bi-atch' your 'nine'. She'll giggle like a schoolgirl all afternoon.

The Minister for Primary Industry

Stick to traditional bush gear: akubra, checked shirt and a pair of moleskins around your ankles. On no account order a 'just a latte'.

Kim Jong Il

Protective body armour is the way to go for a state dinner with the Dear Leader. Kimmo himself is as gentle as a lamb, but his ravenous staff are likely to attempt to bite into your tasty, fleshy torso if you turn your back on them for a second.

Sauron, the Unblinking Eye of Mordor

Something lightweight and casual. Go for the breezy Don Johnson *Miami Vice* look: linen suit, sleeves rolled up, espadrilles and pastel shirts are best for an al fresco lunch by the furnaces of Mount Doom.

Dress for Success

You've been elected to something. Somehow you've convinced a sizeable group of Australians that you can be trusted with legislative power. Forget about the maiden speech – it's what you wear that really counts. Your sartorial skills are the gateway to a long career in politics. Select your wardrobe carefully before you do anything stupid.

WRONG. Barely acceptable even in Adelaide in the seventies – which it isn't right now, in case you hadn't noticed. Don Dunstan had good legs and pert buttocks, and despite or possibly because of this, he was nearly killed by PCP-crazed bikies in Hindley Street when he showed up for work in these flesh-coloured hotpants.

You're on the right track here. Just don't wear this get-up in front of a TV camera or there'll be numerous spontaneous incidents of epilepsy out there in television land.

Get rid of the glasses, get your teeth done, do something about those eyebrows and would it kill you to wear a tie?

Better, but still a long way to go . . .

There's no point trying to make strawberry jam out of sheep shit. Billy Snedden understood this implicitly. He knew he was an idiot of the highest order and saw no point in disguising the fact.

Standing in front of a rostrum with a few flags in the background screams authority. Just make sure it's the Australian flag, okay?

Erm . . . Too much.

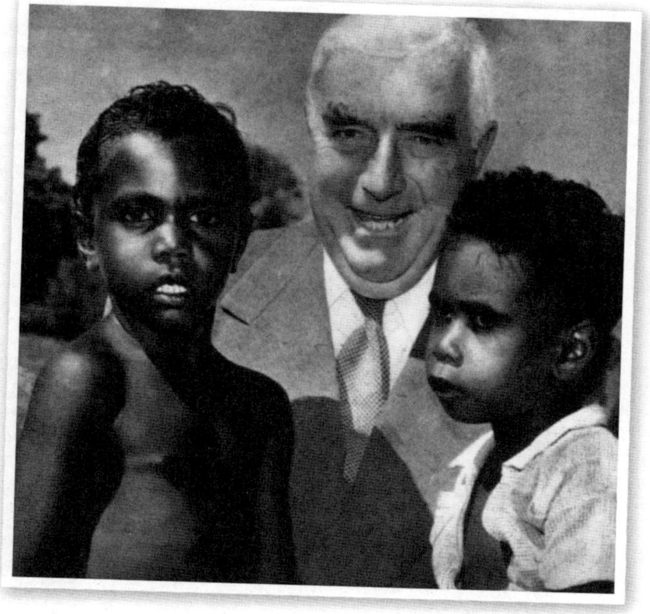

Now this oozes authority. Menzies is grinning paternalistically, as if to say 'I have these kids' lives in the palm of my hand. Better ship them off to some ghastly institution before I catch something nasty from them, eh?' Pretending you care about the dispossessed while never really giving a shit about them will ensure you'll always be deeply admired by the electorate at large.

For some, a nice suit and gigantic shoes are the way to go.

This is a lot better. Putting on a wetsuit and biting the heads off fish shows the electorate that you're a man of action. Just watch out for that rip . . .

Nothing says you're leadership material more than sporting a blazer with the word 'Australia' printed on it a couple of hundred times. Suitable for a day at the races or a 48-hour drinking binge on the taxpayer.

You've made it. Normally old men wearing tracksuits is an unforgivable fashion faux pas but politics is a strange game. Just make sure it's green and gold and bears the moniker of the Australian team du jour. This bloke never gets it wrong.
NB: It's five o'clock in the morning and MP for Eden-Monaro Gary Nairn, left, is wearing a cravat. Keep an eye on him. The guy is going places.

SPOT ON. Not much doubt about who's the dominant figure in the room when you stroll into the chamber with a bit of ceremonial headgear from PNG. Keating had to kill seven Papuan highlanders and drink blood from their penis gourds before he was allowed to wear this.
When in Melbourne watch out for tramlines.

Jack's Conclusion

You're just about done. I've given you the tools you need, the keys to the kingdom. You've squeezed me dry of everything I know and I'm lying here on the floor in a puddle of my own urine. I've barely got enough energy to raise my arm to pen these few words and to sign the invoice from the bottle shop.

Fidler! Make me a mint julep and don't fuck around. Then come here and rub my feet. Ah, yes that's the spot. Work between the toes, there's a good lad.

Christ, I'm parched.

You've taken it all from me. The petrol gauge is flickering around the 'E' sign and I'll need to have a very large surf'n'turf and several buckets of amber nectar to recover.

I've given you the secret maps of power in this great country. Now it's time for you to go out into the nation and tear off a large chunk for yourself and say 'mine!'

Then buy me a drink. And make it a large one. A man can barely get his gob damp with a schooner these days. Are they making them smaller now, I wonder? Knocking them out with thicker glass to cheat a man of some much needed fluids. I wouldn't put it past the bastards. There's no end to their deception. I blame the Rechabites. They've always had it in for me . . .

Afterword

I have called my friends at the Cooperative who have urged me to go on strike and stay on strike until such a time as the publishers withdraw this book from the shelves and pulp the pages into a slurry. The dross can then be fed to endangered tree frogs and other nurturing pouched marsupials of like mind.

At least then some good may come of this low-brow, lightweight affront to those who seek to confront the male-dominated, meat-eating (MEAT = MURDER) power structure. I deplore this book's celebration of the fascist State – with its whole ancient and dismal apparatus of jails, armies, and armed robbery (TAXATION = COERCION); with all its death, its sponsored diseases (SILENCE = DEATH); with all its grotesque and repressive legislation and military attempts (BUSH = LIES), internal and external, to interfere with the Sisterhood and our freely chosen cooperative ventures, selling on a not-for-profit basis non-penile penis prostheses.

I am going now. No, no, that's my last word on the subject …

Glossary

Adams, Dick: Much loved federal MP for the Tasmanian seat of Lyons. The only Richard in Australia still happy to be called 'Dick' by complete strangers.

Barons: The last decent place to get a drink in Kings Cross. Now closed.

Barwick, Sir Garfield: Chief justice of the High Court (1964–81), and attorney-general in the Menzies Government. Fondly remembered as the first chief justice to give tax cheaters a much deserved break.

Beard: Pubic hair that heads north for a drink. Also, a female companion partnered by an obviously gay man to dispel the perception that he is a shirt lifter.

Bold Personality: *See* Fine Cotton.

Bradman, Don: Freemason who thought Australian cricketers should be happy representing their country for the price of a ham sandwich and a packet of Twisties. Good at batting but not much else.

Burgess, Baby John: Sartorially perfect former ten-pin bowling champ, and host of *Wheel of Fortune* and *Burgo's Catchphrase.*

Burner: An aeroplane; often used to transport vast mineral wealth from Australia to China.

Cahill Expressway: Elegant, elevated public carriageway constructed above Circular Quay to prevent common people looking at Sydney Harbour.

Callinan, Ian: Retired High Court justice. Took up 'judgin' when disappointing sales of his erotic novels failed to provide him with a living. Required by the constitution to step down in September 2007 at age of seventy; a provision often criticised for depriving the court of people of the calibre of Kamahl and Bruce Ruxton.

Cane Toad: Australia's national amphibian.

Cass, Moss: Former environment minister in the Whitlam Government. Widely considered to be a 'spunk' by female Labor apparatchiks for his beard-without-the-moustache look. Suspected of having stolen Max Walker's leftover facial hair.

Connie Jacket: Lightweight black cardigan banded by a red stripe. Favoured by original Melbourne skinheads of the seventies.

Connor, Rex 'the Strangler': Minister for minerals and energy in the Whitlam Government, 1972–1975. The last Australian politician to wear a hat in public until John Howard embarrassed the nation more than two decades later.

Corowa: Charming historic town on the River Murray with ninety-eight pubs and no toilets. Site of a crucial constitutional convention which led to the founding of the Australian nation in 1901.

Crean, Frank: Treasurer in the Whitlam Government. Believed to have said that he could fix the economy if he could only find his glasses. Simon's dad.

Crème de Menthe: A refreshing, minty beverage. You need to be drunk before you can even begin to consume this superlative cordial.

Crown and Anchor: A dice game favoured by Jack at smoke nights. In 1974, after an astonishing roll of thirty-six anchors in a row, Jack became the wealthiest man in the world, just pipping the Aga Khan. He lost it all at the Sandown greyhounds the following night.

Dangerfield, Rodney: The greatest stand-up comedian. Ever.

Dapto Dogs: The Mecca of coursing in this country and what's more, a top night out for all the family. *See also* Dishlickers.

Delmonti: The makers of the finest black suits in the whole, wide world. Demand for Delmonti suits went through the roof in the eighties after Hal Todd's famous ad with the slogan *Delmonti suits: look good, feel good, ARE good.*

Dishlickers, Dishies, 'Lickers: Pointy-faced little horses who run around a track for the amusement of the gaming and wagering community. A dab of English mustard on their dates makes them go faster.

Fine Cotton: A picnic meeting nag who rose to fame in 1984 by bravely winning against the odds at a midweek meeting at Eagle Farm. The injudicious intervention of the stewards saw Fine Cotton disqualified and millions of punters did their dough. Jack maintains that crucial DNA evidence will one day 'sort this whole business out, once and for all'.

Fowler, Graham 'Chook': Former New South Wales police detective and selfless warrior for justice. Tragically forced to retire after 'slipping on a milkshake'; an incident he eerily predicted on an anti-corruption surveillance tape only the day before. Thought to have mind-bending precognitive powers.

Fraser, Malcolm: Australian prime minister (1975–83). Sought power with a ruthlessness that almost provoked civil war in this country. Once in power he governed like a craven idiot. Won office because the Whitlam Government had presided over a recession, then drove the country into an even worse one. Fraser is now a leading campaigner for niceness in public life.

Gair, Vince: Labor premier of Queensland (1952–57). Expelled from the ALP in the great split of the fifties and subsequently elected as a DLP senator. In 1974 the Whitlam Government offered him the position of ambassador to Ireland and the Holy See. However Gair was distracted from officially resigning that night, drinking beer and eating prawns with several Country Party senators in a sting that became known as 'The Night of the Long Prawns'.

Gilmore, Mary: Australian poet and writer. Moved to Paraguay to form a utopian socialist colony with a group of journalists. Left the colony just before its inhabitants were reduced to murder and cannibalism. Her pretty face was later printed on a ten pound note.

Henley Beach: Seaside Adelaide suburb where FM radio hosts hand out icy-cold cans of Coke from a Black Thunder bus.

Hinze, Russ: Minister for everything in Queensland's Bjelke-Petersen Government. A large man with a large appetite, Hinze needed to ingest six horses a day, just to survive. Cheerfully tossed aside accusations of conflict of interest.

Holt, Harold: Australian prime minister (1966–67). Went for a swim without his floaties and never came back. The Victorian Government later tastelessly built a public swimming pool in his name as a memorial to him.

Jackson, Rex 'Buckets': Noted prison reformer in New South Wales who believed that the best place for criminals was back on the streets. Shocked to discover that Arthur 'Neddy' Smith was a recidivist, Jackson was forced to resign from the Wran Government and get stuck into a little prison reform at the coalface.

Kelly, Paul: The nation's leading political commentator. Holds the title of 'Editor-at-Large' at *The Australian*, which means he's wanted for crimes against print journalism. Kelly's mind is powered by PowerPoint software, which means he can only write and talk in dot points.

Kelly, Ray: Brilliant New South Wales police detective, able to exercise his own brand of justice unburdened by the dead hand of judicial oversight.

Kerr, Sir John: Former governor-general of Australia. Hated by 42.4 per cent of the country after his dismissal of the Whitlam Government. Salvaged his reputation by making a pass at Diamond Jim McLelland and falling over drunk at the Melbourne Cup.

Khemlani, Tirath 'Old Rice and Monkey Nuts': International banking genius who fell in with Rex 'The Strangler' Connor, delighting the old Labor salt with magic tricks, making coins disappear and reappear again. Deeply impressed, the Strangler asked Khemlani if he could lend him three billion dollars.

Krahe, Fred: Fearless guardian of law and order in New South Wales. A copper who got the job done by exhaustive investigative process, surgical interrogation technique and a set of boltcutters. Dead now. *See also* Spanish.

Leger, to salute at the: The finishing post at a racetrack. The dwarf atop a thousand pounds of dangerously stupid beast who crosses the finish line first is said to salute at the leger.

Lewis, Terry: Former Queensland police commissioner. In 1989 'Sir Terrence' was found guilty of accepting bribes totalling a mere seven hundred large from brothels, SP bookies and illegal casinos. After his release from prison he showed bucketloads of spunk by asking for a substantial handout from the Queensland State Government.

Lindrum, Walter: An uncanny genius at billiards, snooker and Hungry, Hungry Hippos. A great Australian.

Lobby Loyde and the Coloured Balls: The greatest Australian band of all time.

Mandarine Napoléon: A brandy flavoured with mandarin rind, designed to induce maudlin feelings in alcoholics by reminding them of the playground lunches of their childhood.

Maralinga: A region in South Australia famous for its cracker nights in the 1950s. Future site of Australia's hot rocks industry.

McEwen, 'Black Jack': Country Party leader who served as interim prime minister of Australia (December 1967 – January 1968) after the death of Harold Holt. As minister for trade and industry in the post-war era he raised the tariff wall so high that only Himalayan Sherpas could scale it.

McHale, Jock: Collingwood footy coach and player. He coached Collingwood between 1797 and 1980, unable to extricate himself from an onerous and deeply binding contract knocked up by John Wren.

Monash, Sir John: Outstanding military commander of World War I and prominent Jewish mailman.

Mossop, Rex: Former Wallaby, rugby league commentator and host of *Controversy Corner*. As a broadcaster, Rex 'The Moose' Mossop was particularly admired for tautologies such as, 'If I keep getting Boyd and O'Grady mixed up, it's because they look alike, especially around the head.'

Oxford: Unit of currency. One Oxford scholar equals a dollar.

Phar Lap: The god of horses. Copped a hot shot after falling out with some colourful Italian-American racing identities.

Richo: Graham Richardson. Toiler's friend and former intimate of Bob Hawke, Paul Keating, Kerry Packer and Rene Rivkin.

Romper Room: Massively popular children's television show screened on the Seven Network. Co-hosted by Miss Marilyn and a Mr Do-Bee: a hateful, sanctimonious puppet who can shove his smug life lessons up his tiny insectoid arse.

Rundle Mall: Built with South Australian premier Don Dunstan's own two hands in the 1970s as a place where South Australians could meet. Possibly the most dangerous place in the world.

Sigley, Ernie: Host of enormously popular Nine Network variety series *The Ernie Sigley Show* (1974–76). The little Aussie battler began his career with *In Adelaide Tonight*, which ran between 8.05 and 8.07 of an evening in the sixties, until it was replaced with a beer ad.

Silvertex: Al Grassby's tailor of choice and a fine haberdasher, falling just short of the world's finest makers of black suits, Delmonti. Rose to fame with the happy motto: *It's a great bag of fruit, it's a Silvertex suit.*

Singo, John Singleton: Advertising genius who managed the difficult feat of selling beer and Bob Hawke to Australians. Bold defender of meek and helpless citizens like Alan Jones.

Skull Bong: A hookah fashioned from a human skull.

Smoke Night, Pie Night: Spectacular soiree where cocktail saveloys and party pies are served in between burlesque enetertainment and a roll of the dice on the Crown and Anchor tables, often held for the benefit of retiring High Court justices.

Spanish, Spanish Dancer: Cancer. Tumours the size of footballs in your guts. When you've got Spanish there's no point buying that five-year diary you've had your eye on.

Swagman, The: Outstanding cultural centre in Melbourne's outer suburbs. Mysteriously burst into flames in the 1980s, leaving the people of Melbourne without a decent smorgasbord and floor show to this day.

Tapp, Johnnie: Race caller and an eerily good judge of equine flesh. A doyen of the thoroughbred racing caper and the only broadcaster in Australia worth the candle. A great Australian.

Taxi Club: Superior late-night entertainment establishment in Sydney's gay precinct. A place where a conflicted Jehovah's Witness could go to be felt up by a 60-year-old transsexual cabbie in peace.

Tuckey, Wilson: Senior Liberal MP for the regional WA seat of O'Connor. A sensitive and thoughtful public servant, he received the nickname 'Iron Bar' after being convicted of assaulting an Aboriginal man with a length of steel cable.

Victorian Racing Club: A bunch of threepenny pissants. I wouldn't give them the steam off my piss.

Viscount: Jack the Insider's preferred brand of cancer stick.

Wrest Point Casino: Cylindrical gaming establishment on the edge of the Derwent River in Tasmania. Opened in 1973 as Australia's first legal casino. A place where you can eat handfuls of prawns, drink a Kahlua and milk and yank away at a one-armed bandit – all at the same time.

Youngman, Henny: Beloved American stand-up comedian. Revolutionised comedy with his invention of the *Take my wife... please!* joke. Made brief cameo performance in Martin Scorsese's *Goodfellas.*

Jack's Acknowledgements

If I have seen further it is because I have been standing on the shoulders of giants. In some cases those giants have been aged cripples with rheumatoid arthritis, but I climbed up their backs for a good look anyway.

Pope Benedict was enormously helpful on the secret rituals of the Vatican. He's been on the phone since then begging me to take him out for a pie night when he's next in Australia. Benny, if you're reading this, stop calling me: you're giving my girlfriend the shits. And, I suspect, yours as well.

Little Johnnie Howard was terrific too. I saw him repeatedly at Kirribilli House throughout 2007; we chatted the hours away while he dug a bunker under the floorboards, preparing for the day when his enemies, the lesbian schoolteachers who run the country, would come and tell him to leave.

Kevvy Rudd tried his best to be helpful. I asked him for an interview; two days later he sent me the interview with his answers and his questions as well. Nobody likes a smartarse, Kevvy.

I had a mongrel of a time tracking down **Osama bin Laden** . . . but I did it. After months of searching, I was blindfolded and stuffed in the back of a car for two hours, then taken into a nondescript tent in Waziristan. And there he was: sitting on the ground, eating some camel fat on a Sao biscuit. It was at that moment I realised I'd forgotten my Arab–English phrasebook.

But I picked up the gist of what he was trying to say. It turns out the scourge of the Western world is a big Collingwood supporter (wouldn't you know it?). He was deeply concerned about their late season form slump. Osama had harsh things to say about Mickey Malthouse, but I told him Nathan Buckley should get out of the way for a younger, fitter captain and he hit the roof. Twenty soldiers reached for their guns but I didn't back down. I said I'll be fucked if I'll be lectured on Collingwood by a bearded nabob living miles away from the MCG. He calmed down and then treated me to a panegyric on South Australia during the Dunstan years. His deep insights were invaluable.

For **Peter Hoysted** and **Richard Fidler** I have nothing but contempt. Neither of these clowns can type, or write shorthand, and they both knocked back my tender sexual advances made in a moment of alcoholic weakness. Get fucked the pair of you.

Finally I couldn't have written a word without the constant help, advice and humour of **Jean-Paul Sartre.** I keep the severed head of JPS in a big glass jar in my garage, plugged into my old black and white AWA television. Through this remarkable device, Jean-Paul was able to read my early drafts. He was also able to communicate his grave misgivings about the future of harness racing in Australia. This is to be the subject of a forthcoming book on this important subject.

Further Acknowledgements

The authors would like to thank Bruce Venables for his poem 'Bin Night', which appears on pages 100–101.

Random House Australia would like to thank Getty Images, Fairfax Photos, AAP Image, Newspix, Jupiterimages, AUSPIC, the National Library of Australia, the National Archives of Australia, Flinders University Library, the High Court of Australia and The Flag Institute for their help with the illustrations and photographs which appear in this book.

Photographs and Illustrations: Sources and Credits

Front cover photograph
Jack the Insider: Bill Chan and Peter Hoysted

Back cover photographs
Former Australian prime ministers with Queen Elizabeth: Paul Harris, Fairfax Photos
Gough Whitlam at Old Parliament House: National Library of Australia
Bush Hosts Dinner for Australia's Howard: Getty Images
The Dalai Lama in Costa Rica: Mayela Lopez, AFP/AAP Image
John Howard with Air Marshall Angus Huston in Iraq: Andrew Taylor, Fairfax Photos

Flags
Chapter header and background: Flag of Australia, Stockbyte, Getty Images
Flag illustrations in chapters 1 and 3: courtesy of The Flag Institute

Illustrations listed by page number
xiii *The Romans of the Decadence*, 1847: Thomas Couture, The Bridgeman Art Library, Getty Images
3 Big Bang illustration: Antonio M. Rosario, The Image Bank, Getty Images
5 Captain Cook: National Library of Australia
8 Henry Lawson: National Library of Australia
Alfred Deakin: AUSPIC
11 *The Queen Shows the Royal Collection,* painting by Josefine Swoboda: Tim Graham Photo Library, Getty Images
12 Amanda Vanstone: Andrew Taylor, Fairfax Photos
14 The Senate and the House of Representatives: AUSPIC
17 John Kerr: Fairfax Photos
18 Anterior view of the male body: 3D4Medical.com, Getty Images
23 Australian Coat of Arms: Neil Duncan, Photolibrary
27 Gothic tree: R.C. Applegate, Stock.XCHNG
28 Bob Hawke: Newspix
30 Barry Jones: Peter Morris, Fairfax Photos
Gareth Evans: AUSPIC
Dick Adams: Alan Porritt, AAP Image
Moss Cass: AUSPIC
Don Dunstan: News Ltd, Dunstan Collection, Flinders University Library
31 Kevin Rudd: Ian Waldie, Getty Images
32 John Howard: Jason South, Fairfax Photos
33 John Howard: Nick Laham, Getty Images
35 David Flint: Sam Mooy, AAP Image
36 Cattle: Alberto Incrocci, The Image Bank, Getty Images
37 Mark Vaile: Ian Waldie, Getty Images
38 Bob Brown: Regis Martin, Getty Images
Steve and Susan Fielding: John Woudstra, Fairfax Photos
Pauline Hanson: Robert Rough, Fairfax Photos
39 Ben Chifley: AUSPIC
40 Edmund Barton: Hulton Archive, Getty Images
Billy Hughes: AUSPIC
John Curtin: Hulton Archive, Getty Images
Ben Chifley: AUSPIC
Robert Menzies: Reg Birkett, Hulton Archive, Getty Images
41 Billy McMahon: AUSPIC
Malcolm Fraser: Central Press/Hulton Archive, Getty Images
Bob Hawke: Patrick Riviere, Getty Images
Paul Keating: Patrick Riviere, Getty Images
John Howard: Paul Harris, Fairfax Photos
43 *The Haywain, Allegory of the Vanity of the World*: Workshop of Gillis Mostaert, The Bridgeman Art Library, Getty Images
Parliament House: Rob Homer, Fairfax Photos
46 George W. Bush: Alan Porritt, AAP Image
48 George W. Bush: Darren McCollester, Getty Images
51 Robert Askin: Robert Pearce, Fairfax Photos
53 Go Go dancers: Michael Ochs Archives, Getty Images
54 Michelangelo's *David*: David Silverman, Getty Images
55 Burdekin Dam: Bryan Lynch, Newspix
56 Joh Bjelke-Petersen: Peter Solness, Fairfax Photos
57 Mike Rann and Claire Martin: Steve Strike, AAP Image

58 Burial site, North Salisbury, Adelaide: Dallas Kilponen, Fairfax Photos
59 Nimbin commune: Fairfax Photos
61 Henry Bolte: Newspix
63 Open cast mining, Brazil: Tim Graham Photo Library, Getty Images
64 Brian Burke: Erin Jonasson, Fairfax Photos
65 Prince Aga Khan: Laurent Rebours, AP/AAP Image
67 Bombing of Darwin: Newspix
68 King Penguin colony: Colin Monteath/Hedgehog House, Minden Pictures, Getty Images
69 Colleen McCullough: Quentin Jones, Fairfax Photos
79 Phillip Adams: Patrick Riviere, Getty Images
81 Alan Jones: Wade Laube, Fairfax Photos
84 John Laws: Dean Lewins, AAP Image
86 Eddie McGuire: Lindsay Moller, Newspix
92 Ray Martin: Patrick Riviere, Getty Images
Kerry O'Brien: Fairfax Photos
Laurie Oakes: Penny Bradfield, Fairfax Photos
Tony Jones: Andy Baker, Newspix
93 Lee Lin Chin, Anna Coren, Melissa Doyle and David Koch: Patrick Riviere, Getty Images
Andrew G and James Mathison: Janie Barrett, Fairfax Photos
95 Steve Irwin: Justin Sullivan, Getty Images
104 Painting by Adolf Hitler: Todd Buchanan, Time & Life Pictures/Getty Images
107 Ingmar Bergman: AAP Image
108 Paul McCartney: Fairfax Photos
111 Adam Smith: Getty Images
112 Wilson Tuckey: David Tease, Fairfax Photos
113 Brick wall: Stock.XCHNG
114 Hannibal Lecter: Universal Pictures, AAP Image
115 Peter Costello: Alan Porritt, AAP Image
116 A Chinese worker fixes power cables in central Beijing: Teh Eng Koon, AFP/Getty Images
121 Allan Moss: Paul Jones, Fairfax Photos
123 Richard Branson: Patrick Riviere, Getty Images
127 Garfield Barwick: National Library of Australia
128 Opening of the first High Court in Melbourne: National Library of Australia
129 Full bench of the Australian High Court: Michael Jones, Newspix
130 High Court justices: courtesy of High Court of Australia
133 Roger Rogerson: Newspix
136 Stanley Bruce: Underwood & Underwood, Time & Life Pictures/Getty Images
138 Fidel Castro: AFP/Getty Images
Robert Mugabe: AP/AAP Image
Kim Jong Il: AFP/Getty Images
Osama bin Laden: http://cenlaugh.wordpress.com
Hugo Chavez and Mahmoud Ahmadinejad: Atta Kenare, AFP/AAP Image
142 Daniel Mannix: Aral, Time & Life Pictures/Getty Images
143 Pope Benedict XVI: Filippo Monteforte, AFP/Getty Images
145 Rowan Williams, Archbishop of Canterbury: Leon Neal, AFP/Getty Images
146 Ayman al-Zawahiri: AFP/Getty Images
147 Man on camel: Frederick Goodall, www.goodallartists.ca
150 Dalai Lama: Craig Sillitoe, Fairfax Photos
151 Bill Harrigan: Colin Whelan, Action Photographics/AAP Image
152 Brian Houston: Bryan O'Brien, Fairfax Photos
153 Alien: Jupiterimages
154 Jim Taylor: AP/AAP Image
155 Gordon Hinckley: Douglas C. Pizac, AP/AAP Image
156 A.C. Bhaktivedanta Swami Prabhupada: Keystone, Hulton Archive, Getty Images
157 Crowds at a Jainist festival: James Burke, Time & Life Pictures/Getty Images
158 Iran – Festival of Fire: Atta Kenare, AFP/AAP Image
159 Stone: Constantin Jurcut, Stock.XCHNG
160 Bindi Irwin: Janie Barrett, Fairfax Photos
161 *Satan in Council*, from Book I of *Paradise Lost* by John Milton, engraved by Stephane Pannemaker: After Gustave Dore, The Bridgeman Art Library, Getty Images
162 Man with puzzled expression: Daniel Arsenault, Riser/Getty Images
165 National Tally Room: Ray Strange, Newspix
169 Gough Whitlam, 1972: Rick Stevens, Fairfax Photos
170 Gough Whitlam with Mekeo dancers: Rick Stevens, Fairfax Photos
171 Gough Whitlam, 1975: Michael Jensen, National Library of Australia
172 Bob Hawke, 1983: Lorrie Graham, Fairfax Photos
173 John Howard, 1987: National Archives of Australia
174 Paul Keating, 1993: Julian Zakaras, AFP/Getty Images
175 John Howard, 1996: Rick Rycroft, AP/AAP Image
176 Kim Beazley, 1998: Mal Fairclough, AP/AAP Image
177 Children overboard: Newspix
178 Mark Latham and John Howard: Penny Bradfield, Fairfax Photos
186 Philip Ruddock (top): Sandy Scheltema, Fairfax Photos
Philip Ruddock (bottom): Robert Pearce, Fairfax Photos
187 Philip Ruddock and John Howard: Alan Porritt, AAP Image
Philip Ruddock: David Hancock, AFP/Getty Images
189 Don Dunstan: Dunstan Collection, Flinders University Library
190 Al Grassby: Newspix
John Howard: Fairfax Photos
191 John Howard: Peter Morris, Fairfax Photos
Billy Snedden, Newspix
192 Alexander Downer: Nick Wass, AP/AAP Image
Pauline Hanson: Dallas Kilponen, Fairfax Photos
193 Robert Menzies with two Aboriginal children, on the cover of *Dawn* magazine, August 1958: www1.aiatsis.gov.au/dawn/docs/v07/s08/1.pdf
Andrew Peacock: Peter Rae, Fairfax photos
194 Harold Holt: Jody D'Arcy, Newspix
Bob Hawke: Fairfax Photos
195 John Howard: John Feder, Newspix
Paul Keating with representatives of the Oro people in Papua New Guinea: Andrew Taylor, Fairfax Photos

About the Authors

Richard Fidler is a writer and broadcaster who presents *The Conversation Hour* on ABC Local Radio on 702 ABC Sydney and 612 ABC Brisbane. He is a former member of comedy trio the Doug Anthony Allstars and as part of that group performed all over the world and co-hosted shows for ABC TV, the BBC and Channel 4. Since then he has presented TV series on science, documentaries and the arts, including *Race Around the World*, *Aftershock* and *The Hub*.

Richard first met Jack the Insider in Buenos Aires. The friendship was cemented back in Australia, when Richard called upon Jack's services to fix up a few zoning difficulties he was having with his holiday house, and to destroy the reputation of the twenty people who were ahead of him in the queue to fill in for Tony Delroy on ABC Radio.

Peter Hoysted is an author and humorist who never quite cut it as a true crime writer. He appears as a regular columnist on Richard Fidler's afternoon program on ABC Radio Queensland. His drunken ramblings have appeared in the pages of *The Australian*, *The Sydney Morning Herald* and in other pornographic publications, in between the pink bits.

He is dedicated to making the world a sillier place.